Homes from Home

Homes from Home

INVENTIVE SMALL SPACES, FROM CHIC SHACKS TO CABINS AND CARAVANS

VINNY LEE

jacqui
small

COUNTRY LIVING
MAGAZINE

First published in 2013 by
Jacqui Small LLP
An imprint of Aurum Press
74–77 White Lion Street
London N1 9PF

First published in the USA in 2013

Publisher: Jacqui Small
Managing Editor: Lydia Halliday
Designer: Ashley Western
Editor: Sian Parkhouse
Picture Researcher: Claire Hamilton
Production: Peter Colley

ISBN: 978 1 906417 98 7

A catalogue record for this book is available from the British Library.

2015 2014 2013
10 9 8 7 6 5 4 3 2 1

Printed in China

CONTENTS

Keeping life simple

KEEPING LIFE SIMPLE

There is something special about a small, intimate living space, a place where you can let your imagination roam and where responsibilities are few and far between. Free up your mind and spirit to enjoy the relaxation and simplicity of these places.

Huts and tents, caravans and treehouses are all designed to give the essential comforts of shelter and protection, but without the responsibilities and obligations of a full-time home. If they are permanent, cabins and shacks usually reflect the environment in which they are constructed, with walls of local stone, wood, grass or clay. As they are built from materials found in the vicinity they are naturally sympathetic to the landscape and in time, when the patina of age and a covering of moss and lichen dulls any newness, they almost become part of it.

Traditionally, the structure and design of these small buildings was basic: often one room with a fireplace or stove for warmth and cooking; a bed or platform that would double as a seat as well as a place to sleep; and a rudimentary scrubbed wood table and a couple of stools. Storage was usually in boxes or trunks, easy to move and stack because space was at a premium. And because space was limited and life for the original homeowners was hard, there was no room or money for anything that wasn't a necessity.

If they are mobile, these types of dwellings are specifically designed to be lightweight and portable. Many have historic roots and are copies or reinterpretations of the homes of nomadic tribespeople, or those whose occupations called for them to go from one area to another. For example, yurts have been used since the thirteenth century by the Turkic nomads of the Steppes of central Asia and a similar structure called a ger has been home to many generations of Mongolian tribes. The yurt frame is constructed from steam-bent wooden roof ribs attached to a circular lattice wall. The top of the frame is secured by a tension band, which prevents the ribs from spreading. Over this is laid a covering of layers of felted sheep's wool that insulates the interior and, because of the natural lanolin in the wool, is also waterproof.

Another influential design comes from the Native American tipi, a conical tent frame covered with buffalo skins. These were used by the nomadic hunting tribes, whereas the

Opposite *Centuries-old building techniques, such as interlocking roughly hewn logs, are still employed to construct durable and comfortable retreats that blend in with their woodland settings.*
Above *This contemporary cabin uses the same basic building materials, but in the form of machine-milled planks that are fixed to a frame to create a lightweight, modern building that also blends in with its surroundings.*

settled agricultural groups of the northwest and east favoured the more permanent wigwam or wickiup, made from bent sapling wood and often covered with bark, or layers of grasses or reeds tied in bundles.

Then 'homes to go' took a new turn when tents were put on wheels. In the eighteenth century wagons were first documented as being used for accommodation, as opposed to just utilized for transporting goods or people, and an early recorded case was a group of French circus performers who were noted as travelling and actually living in their wagons.

As well as the showmen and circus communities, accommodation wagons have also long been the home of the Romani, also known as Gypsies, travellers or tinkers. The Roma vardo is the traditional and almost chocolate-box image that we have of this type of vehicle. The vardo was an elaborately carved and decorated wooden wagon, often richly gilded and dressed with patterns featuring Romani symbols. But these are a thing of the past and are also rare, because it was the custom that when the owner died, his or her vardo and its contents would be burnt. What had been so much a part of their life when living was also their property and domain in death.

Above *A canvas bell tent gives some protection from the weather and inquisitive animals but allows the light of the moon and rising sun, as well as the sounds of rain and wind, to penetrate.* **Opposite** *This yurt-style construction provides a semi-permanent resting place and has a boardwalk pathway as well as a log-burning stove.*

'Man's possessions are his burdens' American Shaker motto

The pioneers who travelled across America, and the Trekboers who trekked in South Africa, did so in covered wagons. The wagon was a canvas frame over a wooden cage secured to a floor-like platform, mounted on a metal frame with wheels and pulled along by a couple of horses or mules. These flimsy structures travelled, usually in groups known as trains, across thousands of miles over mountains and prairies until they reached a safe or unclaimed area of land where their owners and families could stake a claim and settle.

On a smaller scale is the shepherd's or herder's hut, a wooden or tin box-like structure on a firm base with strong axels and cast-iron wheels pulled by horses onto a moor or heath so that a shepherd or stockman could watch over his flock during the lambing or calving season. The shepherd's hut, usually fitted with a small log-burning stove in one corner, was kitchen, bed, dining and sitting room, store and sometimes nursery for weak lambs, all under one roof. Many had a hinged stable door, which would be positioned away from the prevailing wind, so that the shepherd could look out and listen to his flock while being provided with some shelter.

The shepherd's hut was a temporary home for the worker away from the farm, but in recent times even the more permanent farm buildings have been made over into places to get away from it all. Although designed as utilitarian grain stores and hay barns, corrugated metal silos and sheds are now comfortable weekend escapes for desk-bound city dwellers.

Another change of use was facilitated when American Wallace 'Wally' Byam founded the Airstream Company in the 1930s. He took the riveted aluminium body construction more commonly seen in aircraft of the time and used it to create the rounded body for a vacation vehicle that provided a lightweight, stylish and comfortable 'home from home' for a family on the move. It is said that the adolescent Byam had worked as a shepherd and had spent nights in a shepherd's hut with his sleeping bag and a gas stove, giving him the idea for creating a more comfortable travelling trailer.

Our desire to get back to basics in order to experience a change of scene and a simpler lifestyle means that we often take a step back in time, finding inspiration from both home and abroad as well as the past. Childhood has influenced my love of small and transient places to stay. As a toddler I had a wondrous 'house' beneath the kitchen table, constructed from a double-sized bedspread draped over the top of the table and hanging down the sides to make four pink walls. When I was six my father built a 'Wendy House', which sat at the bottom of the garden, complete with glass windows, a table and chairs and bunk beds in which a friend and I could sleep overnight. It was an escape from the confines of the world of grown-ups, and to some extent that is still what we seek in a hideaway or hut.

Even now my idea of a good holiday is not to stay in a five-star luxury hotel but to find a trullo, cabin or bothy that is truly a part of the landscape, history and culture of the area I am visiting. It gives a real feel for how it might be to live somewhere, rather than just visit.

Our lives have become increasing complex and demanding with the constant bombardment of information, speed, traffic and noise. Leave everything but the essentials behind and head, at least for a few weeks a year, to the hills or the beach and get back to basics, free up your mind and spirit and really enjoy the pleasures and leisure of these places.

Opposite *Shepherd's huts used to be moved from flock to flock during the seasons but now they are towed from autumn woodland to spring pasture for the enjoyment of the countryside during its most attractive times.* **Above** *Showman's vans travelled from village fete to town fair, and were a compact 'home from home' for performers and their families.* **Below** *The aluminium-clad recreational vehicle dates from the 1930s.*

SETTING THE MOOD

When you arrive in a new or different environment it can take time to acclimatize and really relax, but undertaking simple tasks or enjoying a favourite pastime will help you settle more quickly and to get the most from the location, and the weather.

TO DO....

Make your own book of walks. Draw landmarks rather than taking photographs. By studying the object you will have a more thorough knowledge than if you take a quick snap.

- -

If you are in the snow try some tracking – follow and identify as many animal and bird prints as you can. They stand out easily against the white background.

- -

Get close up with ice crystals – look at snow under a microscope or magnifying glass and see its myriad formations.

- -

Snow cleaning is a natural alternative to chemically dry cleaning woollen blankets and rugs – and the colder and crisper the weather, the better. Hang the blankets and rugs on a clothesline during a snowfall. When well covered gently brush off the snow, which will remove the surface dirt with it, leaving the cool and fresh blankets and rugs ready to bring back indoors.

- -

Make outdoor ice cubes – drop strips or pinches of edible berries, cloves, dried lemon and orange peel and coriander seeds in egg cups of fresh water. Cover and leave outside overnight.

- -

Hills and mountains

In areas of rolling terrain the landscape will vary from sandy lower levels to angular rocky outcrops, or from heathland and moors to forest-topped hills. There will also be areas of light and shade, heat and coolness, and plant and wildlife will vary, so take time during your first few days to study how the landscape changes, then plan walks and excursions to compare and contrast these zones. On a crisp, clear day you could head for the hilltops and get an overview of the area, while on warmer days you may stay in the low-lying areas and look at more local and immediate points of interest. You can also head to the hills for traditional winter sports, such as snowboarding and skiing

Hilltops are ideal for kite flying, with plenty of uplift and currents, and you will soon become aware of the direction of wind flow. If you haven't got a kite, watch larger birds, such as seagulls or hawks, using the eddies to help them fly.

At twilight find a suitable clearing or patch of open ground and settle down for some stargazing – you will get the best views away from light pollution caused by street lights and buildings. As a basic guide, stars tend to twinkle and planets shine – look for the dominant constellation in your area, for example, the Southern Cross or the Pole Star. You may also see shooting stars and man-made satellites. Don't forget a torch to find your way home and, if you have one, take a telescope or binoculars to get a clearer view of the heavens.

Opposite, above *From a hillside deck you can experience the sky melting from blue to pink and gold, then into blackness with a scattering of silver stars, and the smells of dried grasses and dusty tracks as they merge into the musky scents of log fires and evening scented flowers.* **Opposite, below** *Life in the mountains benefits from fresh, clear air and endless silence.*

Fields and dales

In pastoral or farmland settings the land tends to be more sheltered and protected and therefore cultivated and inhabited. Rather than walk on roads, you may find ancient, well-used pathways set down by herdsmen or travellers skirting around field boundaries and riverbanks connecting one settlement to another. There may also be local produce for sale by the wayside, at the farmer's market or in village shops, so look out for regional cheeses, breads, berry preserves and honey.

Before you set out to explore buy a detailed map (at least 1:50 000 scale) for a look at the geography of the district and a local guidebook that will give you an insight into the history and regional landmarks.

When walking take a notebook and jot down the names of villages on signposts, farms or old houses you pass as well as the names of families buried in the local graveyard, mentioned on plaques or war memorials and see if any of them can still be found on shop signs in the village or are the same as people mentioned in the guidebook – this will give you an idea as to the genealogy and longevity of the area's inhabitants.

Make the most of wide open spaces to empty your head of everyday niggles and concerns; try cloud spotting. Lie in a field or on a grassy hill slope and watch the clouds roll by. There are two aspects to this pastime. One is that you can try and predict the weather, spot fronts and learn the formal names for the various formations. Or you can just lie there and let your imagination go – see a dragon-shaped cloud change in to a galleon or a Roman emperor's head become a leaping dolphin.

TO DO....

Harvest lavender, rosemary and camomile or other wild herbs such as angelica, dry them in the sun and tie in bundles or sew into cotton bags, then put them in clothes drawers and linen presses. Take some back home when you leave and hang them in your wardrobe so that you have a daily reminder of your sun-filled days of leisure and pleasure.

Make fresh teas, tisanes and cordials with edible herbs and berries from the hedgerows. Wild strawberries and blackberries can be picked and infused in hot water. Rosehips make a tasty drink, and are an excellent source of vitamin C.

Opposite, left *Take off in your carvan and find a field to camp in. The open aspect of low-lying land makes it a great place to enjoy stargazing. Lying in the centre of a field and looking up gives you an uninterrupted view of miles of sky, free from street and house light pollution.* **Opposite, right** *Field perimeters are ideal for foraging as they are often edged with berry-laden hedgerows and fruit and nut bushes. Look out for crab apples, damsons and cobnuts.* **Above** *Being on a plain or flat land area without shade can mean that daytime temperatures are high and the sun intense. Surrounding hills can also act as a barrier, preventing the heat from escaping, so make sure you have a canopy to shield you and your camp.*

Woodland and forest

Whether it is the arm-stretching girths of giant redwoods or the suppleness of managed saplings in a glade there is something magical about wandering through the dappled light and rustling branches of woodland. Woods and forests are places of variety and surprise, from the hardy eucalyptus, cedars and needles of evergreen pines to the spectacular colours of deciduous oaks, maples and hickory trees. In dark, damp places the sweetest mushrooms can grow alongside deadly fungi, while spongy mosses and feathery lichens and ferns add to the magical feel.

Traditionally, woods and forests were home to a number of crafts, such as charcoal making. Baskets and small pieces of furniture were also made from pliable green willow or sapling wood. In some countries there are annual woodland celebrations. Throughout northern France there are a number of Fêtes de la Forêt, and in Germany the Black Forest region has Fastnacht or Fasnet to celebrate the lore and crafts of the area.

Above and right *Trees provide an ever changing backdrop – sometimes under a blanket of crisp snow, at others shining from a shower of rain or fresh and bright with a burst of new foliage. But when leaves of deciduous trees turn they provide a brief and glorious golden backdrop, from outdoor meals to games of hide and seek.*

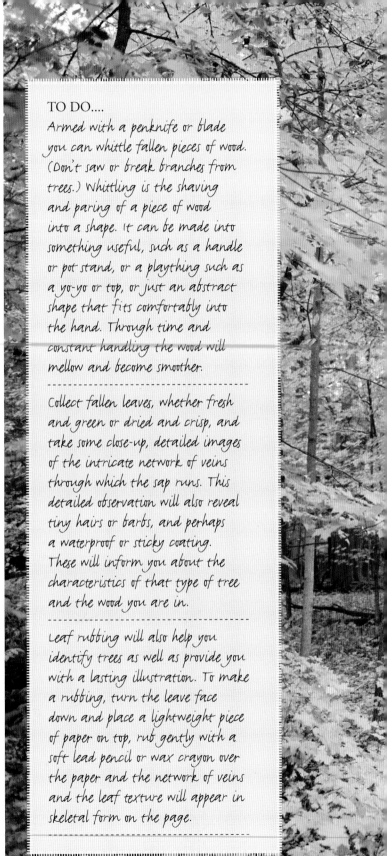

TO DO....

Armed with a penknife or blade you can whittle fallen pieces of wood. (Don't saw or break branches from trees.) Whittling is the shaving and paring of a piece of wood into a shape. It can be made into something useful, such as a handle or pot stand, or a plaything such as a yo-yo or top, or just an abstract shape that fits comfortably into the hand. Through time and constant handling the wood will mellow and become smoother.

Collect fallen leaves, whether fresh and green or dried and crisp, and take some close-up, detailed images of the intricate network of veins through which the sap runs. This detailed observation will also reveal tiny hairs or barbs, and perhaps a waterproof or sticky coating. These will inform you about the characteristics of that type of tree and the wood you are in.

Leaf rubbing will also help you identify trees as well as provide you with a lasting illustration. To make a rubbing, turn the leave face down and place a lightweight piece of paper on top, rub gently with a soft lead pencil or wax crayon over the paper and the network of veins and the leaf texture will appear in skeletal form on the page.

Fresh water

Fresh water, or sweet water as it is sometimes called, is found in streams, rivers and lakes. Fresh water has a low concentration of salts, although it may contain minerals washed from the rocks over which it passes. Freshwater sources are part of the general landscape in which they run or collect, but they generate their own micro-habitats and points of interest. Freshwater lakes can be referred to by regional or local names – for example, in Scotland they are knows as tarns and lochs, in Ireland loughs, in German Sees (as in Bodensee, also known as Lake Constance) and in the southern states of America they are bayous.

If you are on a river you can observe the panorama of the banks as you pass by. Bank watch, especially in the early morning and at dusk: watch holes, dens and burrows in the banks of rivers and lakes for shy creatures such as beavers, otters, platypus and water voles, and among overhanging tree branches for kingfishers, dippers and wagtails. In shallow fresh water you may see fish, such as trout and sticklebacks, as well as insects like the aptly named water boatmen and pond skaters.

Paddle a kayak, canoe or coracle, or if the water is shallow just wade in and watch life on the banks as you drift or paddle through the water – you'll get a more detailed insight into bank life from this angle. But travel lightly and quietly – you don't want to frighten away or disturb the creatures you've come to see.

You can also fish, eat and be merry. In North America they have the clambake; the Portuguese also have their version while in Nordic countries, such as Sweden and Finland, enjoy *kräftskiva* or crayfish parties. First check the local water quality and that you are within the permitted 'harvesting' season, then, if all is clear, pick and catch freshwater mussels, clams and crayfish; all make a delicious base for an outdoor supper.

Opposite and below *Lakes, ponds, rivers and streams are vital for land irrigation and water supply for animals and wildlife so avoid polluting them. The landscape influences how water falls; upland rivers are fast flowing and when travelling over rocks create waterfalls, whereas lowland rivers are slower and meandering. Wetland habitats are ideal for reeds and rushes but also insects, which may bite or sting, so avoid these sites when camping.*

TO DO....

Collect rain in clean containers on deck and use it to wash your hair, and silk or woollen clothes. Rainwater collected in the countryside is softer and has fewer chemicals than tap water. Rainwater is less harsh on the shaft of the hair and on the fibres of wool, cashmere and silk, so wash using a mild shampoo or detergent, rinse thoroughly and dry in the sun for an extra special, soft and sweet-smelling finish.

For your hair, you could try a post-wash rinse of rosemary tonic. Infuse a handful of fresh rosemary in boiling water, leave to cool and strain and then wash through your hair.

The deck of a ship is the ultimate place to lounge and relax, soaking up the sun's rays, ideally with a cold drink at hand. But be extra vigilant about suncream. Sun reflected off water is much stronger.

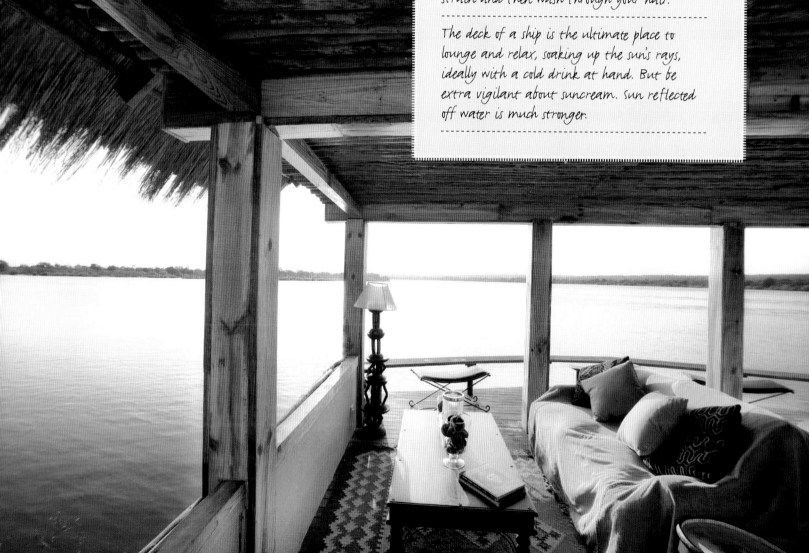

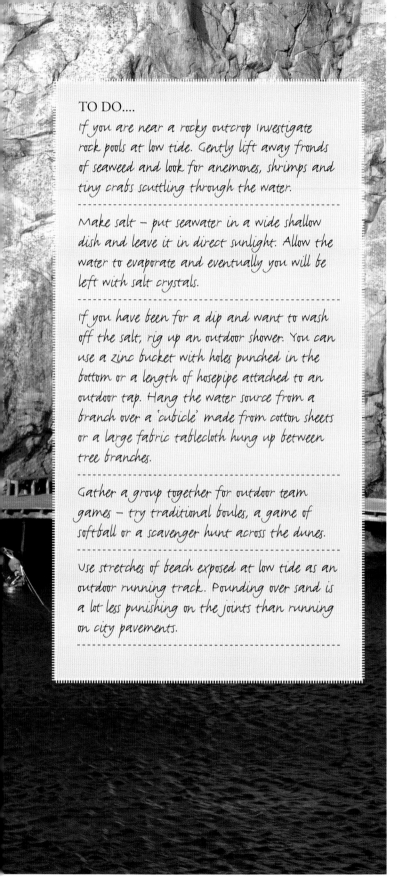

TO DO....

If you are near a rocky outcrop investigate rock pools at low tide. Gently lift away fronds of seaweed and look for anemones, shrimps and tiny crabs scuttling through the water.

Make salt – put seawater in a wide shallow dish and leave it in direct sunlight. Allow the water to evaporate and eventually you will be left with salt crystals.

If you have been for a dip and want to wash off the salt, rig up an outdoor shower. You can use a zinc bucket with holes punched in the bottom or a length of hosepipe attached to an outdoor tap. Hang the water source from a branch over a 'cubicle' made from cotton sheets or a large fabric tablecloth hung up between tree branches.

Gather a group together for outdoor team games – try traditional boules, a game of softball or a scavenger hunt across the dunes.

Use stretches of beach exposed at low tide as an outdoor running track. Pounding over sand is a lot less punishing on the joints than running on city pavements.

Seaside

The wide, seemingly limitless realms of the sea offer untold adventures and treasures. From calm and mirror-like to stormy and foam capped, the sea is an element that demands respect and caution. As Jules Verne puts is 'The sea is everything. It covers seven tenths of the terrestrial globe. Its breath is pure and healthy. It is an immense desert, where man is never lonely, for he feels life stirring on all sides.'

The mood swings of the sea and the effect they have on the coastal land strips that border it mean that it is a constantly changing source of inspiration and fun, from building sandcastles and windsurfing, to fishing and beachcombing. Collect flotsam and jetsam from the beach to recycle and use, perhaps as decorations for your beachside cabin or hut. Make a frame from driftwood, a necklace from smoothed and polished shards of glass, shells or pebbles with holes. If you have a more permanent seaside home then use the things you find to make features and statues in a shingle garden – look at film maker Derek Jarman's at Dungeness in Kent for inspiration.

If you are staying near the sea for a few days or longer map tidal changes. Walk along the shore where you think might be the high tide mark and make a short trail of deep and obvious footprints, or make a series of mounds of pebbles and stones. Come back the next day and see if they have been washed away. If they have, repeat the line of footprints or stones further up the beach until you find that it is still in situ when you return and you will have mapped the limit of the high tide.

We all associate the sea with sunny days, even if our childhood memories are a bit rose-tinted. But the beach can be a playground in all weather. Windy days are great for walking, watching the waves whipped up into white-tipped horses, and activities such as windsurfing, sailing or landsurfing really come into their own. On cooler days you can wrap yourself up in a blanket and settle yourself in a deckchair outside your beach hut to watch the world go by.

Left *The salty sea is volatile and unpredictable; it can be wild and damaging, rotting wood and stripping paint, yet on calm days it is a joy to be around. The weather report becomes an important part of daily life for anyone spending time by the sea.*

PART 1 **HUTS &**

HIDEAWAYS

wood & metal

Opposite *Snugly nestled into a rocky hillside this wooden-clad hideaway is hard to distinguish from its surroundings.* **Above** *A galvanized steel kit house dating from the early 1920s sits unobtrusively in a wildflower meadow. The construction of the house is lightweight but durable and before being restored as a home it was used for a time as a horse's stable.*

Previous pages *Surrounded by indigenous woodland and built out onto the water, this wooden hideaway is secluded, sheltered and enveloped by nature.*

Wood is a widely available material. In its rough, raw state it is often sourced on site, whereas planed and machine finished planks may be worked off-site. Being versatile and lightweight they are easy to transport, as is galvanized sheet metal. Simple, single-storey buildings made from these materials require basic construction skills and minimal manpower to erect, and can be built quickly once the foundation is cleared.

Historians believe that the first log cabins built in America date from the 1630s and were in the Swedish colonies around the Delaware and Brandywine rivers; later German and Ukrainian settlers also used the technique. Log cabins were built from similarly sized tree trunks laid horizontally one on top of another and interlocked at the ends with cog joints or notches. In more recent times these techniques have been replaced with nailing, although purists believe that hammering metal nails into the timber causes weakness in the wood. The weight and careful alignment of the trunks meant that the walls were draughtproof, but where gaps did occur dried mosses were used to infill and insulate.

Although a basic dwelling, the log cabin holds a place at the heart of American culture. Seven presidents of the United States are said to have been born in log cabins, including Abraham Lincoln, Andrew Jackson and James Buchanan. Though not born in one, William Henry Harrison used a log cabin symbol during the 1840 election to show he was a man of the people.

Log cabins are robust and sturdy so are often sited in remote areas where the weather could be harsh. In more sheltered locations wooden buildings were often constructed from sawn planks of wood or small shingle tiles. By overlapping the wooden shingles rainwater and snow would run off the raised bottom end of the

upper layer, therefore protecting the top part of the underlying plank. Woods such as Huon pine, ironbark (a type of eucalyptus), some cypresses and the redwoods are naturally rot resistant and others have resins that provide waterproof protection and insect repellent, so the choice of timber was important.

When freshly cut, wood tends to be rich brown or golden yellow but in time it weathers to subtle hues of grey and silver. Some softer, less resilient woods need to be painted for added protection – for example, in Sweden, Falu red is used for the exteriors of cottages and barns. This paint originated from the copper mines of Falun in the Dalarna region and contains rye flour, linseed oil, iron oxides, copper compounds and zinc. In Finland there is a similar preservative paint known as *punamulta*, which translates as 'red earth'.

Zinc and oxide paints are also used to protect galvanized iron and steel. The development, in the early 1800s, of corrugated iron with its distinctive wavy surface, saw the beginning of an industry exporting 'kit' houses and even churches to countries such as Australia and Jamaica. In Australian and New Zealand some of these tin houses became known as bachs (pronounced 'batches') because they were used as homes for bachelors, and were regarded as being a step above the basher, a shelter built from reclaimed and recycled materials. With time, a stoop or veranda might be added to give a sheltered outdoor space and added protection to the side of the house facing the prevailing elements.

Opposite, clockwise from top left *Some woods have their own subtle scents, which can perfume even the most rustic of rooms. Vines and creepers may envelop a hut or hideaway, but be careful that the tendrils don't invade and damage the structure. Oxide paint protects metal buildings from rusting. When wood has been milled or sawn it will need a coat of paint or varnish to protect the exposed surfaces.*

Log cabins

Wood is a healthy building material because it 'breathes'; it also absorbs sound and is warm and comforting to touch, so helps to create a relaxing and cocooning environment. Traditional log cabins are rectangular, single-storey structures with a pitched roof and walls made from full, round tree trunks, often incorporating a stone or brick chimney and fireplace.

In years gone by wood would be sourced from the nearest forest, but these days it should come from a reputable managed source. After felling the wood must be seasoned to remove excess sap. Unseasoned wood is known as green wood and if used immediately will dry out in situ, moving, twisting and even cracking, therefore making the building liable to harmful settling. Seasoned wood is left to dry on racks in the sunshine and is regularly turned over periods of up to a year, whereas commercial kits often come with kiln- or oven-dried timber that has been quickly and mechanically dried and may still be damp at the core. Seasoned wood is stronger and more stable and, because of the reduction of sap, it is also lighter to transport.

The advantage of log-constructed homes over brick-built houses is that they can be disassembled and transported to a new location and rebuilt. It is also easier to take down a wall and build an extension or addition, with minimal upheaval.

Opposite *Although this cabin is built from logs the chimney has been constructed from stone, which is flame resistant and allows the heat and sparks from the fire to be ducted a safe distance away from the flammable walls and roof shingles.* **Above left** *The steep sides of this roof will improve the run-off of rainwater and also prevent snow building up into thick layers, which could possibly reach a weight that would damage the building's structure.* **Above** *Natural roofing is increasingly popular; sedum and alpine plants need only a thin layer of soil in which to root and will grow to provide good sun protection and insulation.* **Left** *The thick tree trunks used to construct these cabin walls have been left bare as part of the interior, although the infill panels in the ceiling are of milled planks.*

Following pages, left and right *Wood, as a building material, has an affinity with both deciduous woodlands and evergreen forests, blending in with its surroundings. It is also lightweight and easy to transport and may even be airlifted into remote areas by helicopter.*

Planks and shingles

Wood has been an important construction material since humans began building homes and boats. Until the late nineteenth century nearly all boats were made from wood and many of the construction techniques used to build them are related to those found in cabins and huts.

Planks are cut or split from the vertical length of tree trunks and are flat, elongated and rectangular, with parallel faces. Buildings constructed using planks tend to have a more refined, less bulky appearance than log cabins, but require a wooden frame onto which the planks can be attached. Because the wood has been cut and is no longer protected by bark it needs to be treated with a preservative such as tar or paint. Some, made from semi-hardwoods such as sweet chestnut or Douglas fir, can be left natural and as the tannins are weathered out of the timber the wood mellows to a silvery grey.

Commonly found on deck and flooring as well as walls is the tongue and groove system, where each plank has a groove cut along the length of one edge and a protruding ridge or

Below left *This smooth facade has been constructed using a technique similar to carvel boat building, where planks of wood are laid and fixed one on top of another.* **Below** *This overlapping plank structure uses a clinker method, also related to early ship building.* **Opposite, top left** *Sawn wood usually needs to be stained or painted to protect it from damage by water; in the Caribbean it is popular to use bright colours such as these ice cream toned stripes.* **Opposite, top right** *Small tiles of wood, known as shingles, are more adaptable than long planks and allow rounded and erratic shapes to be covered, such as the elegantly curved roof on this unusual cabin.* **Opposite, below** *The vulnerable cut ends of the planks in this building have been given added protection with an upright baton of wood covering the corners.*

tongue on the opposite side. When assembled the tongue from one plank fits into the groove of the other to provide a secure join, often glued for additional strength.

Planks can be used in a variety of ways to create different finishes and effect, such as cladding, or in New Zealand weatherboarding. American houses built using this technique are widely known as clapboard houses, taking the name from the Dutch word *klappen*, which means 'to split'.

Shingles are small, thin slices of split wood, sometimes known as shakes, that are laid like overlapping tiles. They can be formed in simple oblong shapes or more ornate fish-scale styles with a rounded bottom. Often used on roofs, shingles can also be attached, like cladding, to the exterior walls of a wooden-framed house. Shingles are small and versatile so are easily applied to rounded or irregular shapes and in difficult to access areas where a long, rigid plank would not work. Local wood is often used to make shingles because it can withstand local weather conditions and is in keeping with the surroundings; in many areas cedar is a popular choice. Shingles were a popular building material in Scandinavia and were in use up to the 1950s in the countryside. The distinctive roofing and wall patterns found on huts and cabins in some regions of North America are due to the influences of the English, Dutch, German, Scandinavian and French settlers.

Metal cabins

The use of metal sheeting as a building material dates from 1820, when British designer and architect Henry Palmer invented Corrugated Galvanized Iron (CGI), sheets of mild steel, cold rolled to produce a corrugated or wavy pattern. The corrugations increased the pliability of the sheet, which was also lightweight and easily transportable. These properties made CGI the perfect material for prefabricated structures and became the main component for cheap kit-style buildings that were widely exported to Australia, New Zealand, Chile, India and America.

During the Second World War, CGI was used extensively in the manufacture of the half-cylindrical Nissen hut in the United Kingdom and in the United States for the Quonset hut. Many remain in use today and have been adapted from military use to domestic housing and holiday homes. Steel cargo containers, too, have had a makeover for domestic use.

Corrugated metal buildings are generally lightweight so they need to be firmly grounded and secured. Metal buildings also suffer in extremes of temperature, the metal becoming physically hot in bright sunshine and freezing cold when the temperature drops. There can be problems with humidity so good ventilation is essential to prevent dampness and mould.

Decks and verandas

Above *Before laying a deck consider the direction of the planks. If laid in lines across the front of the cabin they will accentuate its width whereas placed in lines leading towards it they will seem to highlight the deck depth. If you have a stunning view you may want to orientate the direction of the planks towards it so that the eye is drawn in that direction*
Above right *Well-spaced, ribbed decking will prevent water-logging and moss growth.*

Even the smallest shack, hut or cabin benefits from a deck, porch or veranda. In fine weather it can be an additional room or a sun shade, protecting not only those who sit on it but also the fabrics and furnishings of the rooms inside, while in bad weather it provides protection and shelter from the elements.

These open-sided but roofed areas around a building are usually made from a raised wooden deck and railings, although in some parts of Australia and the southern states of American ornate, filigree metal work is also popular.

These structures also have a variety of names. 'Veranda' is thought to be the anglicized version of the Hindi words *bahar* meaning 'outside' and *andar* meaning 'inside', so indicating a space that is both indoors and out. In America the word 'stoop' is often used to describe a small porch and this is said to come from the Dutch settlers in the Hudson valley area of New York, who referred to it in their native language as a *stoep*.

As well as providing extra space and shelter the porch is an invaluable recreation area. A swinging or rocking chair can be placed here so you can relax and enjoy the view, or you can gather with friends over a meal and glass of wine or beer.

Left *Stone slabs are often laid to provide a stable, dry base on which a wooden hut or cabin can be erected, and sometimes the stone is carried on beyond the building to create a deck.*

Below *It is useful to lay down an impervious groundsheet or membrane to protect the underside of a wood deck from damp and also to suppress weed growth, which could sprout between the planks. This deck allows you to feel right in the heart of the forest.*

Living spaces

Left *By continuing the plank wood floor from inside out to the deck and installing fold-back doors there is no visible barrier between the indoor and outside living spaces in this charming lakeside wooden cabin. The Adirondack plank chairs have a similar simple and relaxed appearance to the furniture indoors.* **Above** *The natural colour and texture of wooden walls need little decoration, although old hunting trophies or rustic artefacts add to the charm.*

The key things to remember when furnishing a bolthole 'home from home' are to keep it simple and make it comfortable. The whole point of a relaxed space is that you shouldn't have to worry about an occasional tea spill on the sofa or muddy boots on the floor. Choose practical surfaces and sturdy but inexpensive furnishings. Recycle, reclaim or invent furniture, bring well-loved and worn things from your main home or look out in local junk shops and car boot sales.

Floors should be easy to brush and wipe clean but softened with a rug or mat; armchairs and sofas should be supportive yet comfortable enough for an afternoon snooze. If your space is small then adaptability will be important: choose a sofa that doubles as a bed, a stool that can be used as a side table, wall-mounted lights instead of floor-standing ones and built-in storage instead of freestanding pieces.

Go for plain, simple colour schemes rather than fancy or fashionable and try to reflect something of the environment in which you are located. If you open the window to a view of woodland or forest, look for furnishings that are rustic and wooden; if your outlook is over sea or a river, subtle shades of blue and grey are more in keeping than fluorescent pink.

Cooking

In summer you may find that most cooking and eating is done outdoors with barbecues and picnics, but on cool evenings and damp days the kitchen becomes the hub of the home and may well double as a dining area as well.

Small confined spaces tend to become hot and steamy during cooking so ensure that you have good ventilation, whether it is just opening an adjacent window or turning on an extractor fan. In wood and metal buildings it will also be important to protect the areas around the sink, hob and oven.

With wood there is the danger of a flame starting a fire so ensure that wooden panelling is kept at a safe distance from a gas hob or is protected by a glass or tile splashback. The same conditions may also cause wood to dry out and warp. Prolonged exposure to intense heat may also damage a metal wall, so place an insulating panel between the oven or hot plate and the adjacent panel of metal.

Although second-hand furniture is useful for fitting out a holiday home or bolthole, when it comes to kitchen equipment such as refrigerators or stoves it is safest to buy new, or a professionally reconditioned machine with a guarantee.

Some remote locations may not have access to mains electricity so bottled gas may be the only power available for the stove and hob, and water might be from a well or pumped, via a filtration system, from a nearby river or stream so that there will be a limited amount for everyday use. But don't let that worry you – it means that you wash up once a day instead of three times and cook simple meals over an open fire rather than frequently bake elaborate dishes in the oven.

Storage is always at a premium in small buildings but in those made of wood, or with a wooden frame, the beams and rafters can provide useful hanging space, especially in a kitchen where hooks can be easily screwed into the wood, and pots and pans, ladles and sieves suspended from them.

Far left *Preparing meals in a home from home should be easy, and where possible made with fresh local ingredients, therefore the kitchen layout should focus on utilitarian necessities rather than grand or complicated extras. A simple run of storage units with a fridge and stove is more than adequate* **Left** *A built-in window seat along with a table and chairs provide a simple dining area off the kitchen.* **Above** *Old enamel stoves and vintage kitchen equipment can add to the informal and bygone appearance of a shack or hut.* **Right** *In your main home you may opt for a fully fitted, gleaming matching kitchen but in this type of setting a mix-and-match arrangement of freestanding and some fitted units works well.*

Sleeping

If a day of fresh air and activity in the great outdoors isn't enough to make you sleepy then a comfortable and cosy bedroom will. If space is limited then bunk beds and hammocks are an ideal way of doubling up, especially when you have extra guests staying. Hammocks can be taken down and rolled away during the day, leaving the room clear for daytime activities, but there is a knack to getting in and out of them and that needs to be mastered before you start on your night's rest. Trundle or truckle beds, where one slides under the other, are another useful space saver, as is the built-in pull-down or wall bed, which lies flat against the wall or in a cupboard during the daytime.

The traditional type of bed found in old wooden houses is the box bed, literally a bed inside a box. There are many variations on this style, including a bed inside a large decorated wooden cabinet that was popular in sixteenth- and seventeenth-century northern France and Netherlands. Another style is one built in against a wall, with sliding panels, doors or curtains which, when closed, gave the person in bed privacy and warmth. These days, when heating is hopefully more efficient, or getaway homes are only used during the summer months, the once heavy woollen curtains could be replaced with light voiles or nets, which look attractive and would also offer protection against mosquitoes and other insects.

Left *This type of built-in bed makes use of the low head height area under the roof and, traditionally, the panelling provided insulation, making the bed warm and cosy.* **Below far left** *This freestanding metal-framed bed is also slotted into the space in the eaves. The room is also warmed by the heat of the chimney which vents the fire in the hearth below.* **Below left** *Planks of recycled wood were used to build this headboard, the original weathered colours left as part of the patina and decoration of the piece.* **Right** *In huts and cabins, storage is often scarce, so deep drawers in a bed base will provide room to keep spare bed linen.* **Below** *In a multifunctional room curtains will give privacy to someone sleeping if others need to use the kitchen or stoke the stove.*

Beds are by their nature bulky pieces of furniture, but they can be fitted into 'dead' areas of a room; because they are used when we are lying down full head height is not necessary. Sliding the foot or side of a bed under an eave or part of a sloping roof can be a useful space saver.

The area under a bed may also be utilized for storage, using either separate boxes and bags or two sliding drawers on wheels. If bed linen, blankets and duvets are to be stored for any considerable time they should first be laundered and then stored clean in airtight bags or a warm, dry place.

Vintage Beach Hut

This beach hut on the south coast of England is used year round by its owners Claire Fletcher and Peter Quinell and is furnished with a vibrant selection of second-hand furniture and accessories.

The focus has been on decorating this hut with inexpensive but comfortable things. If anything's damaged it can easily be replaced, but these accoutrements also work to make the hut a relaxing and enjoyable place to be. The salty air and strong sunlight take their toll, bleaching, fading and rotting fabrics, so a stash of crocheted blankets from charity shops offers a cheap and colourful way of providing extra warming layers when you want to sit out in the sun but the air is cooled by a spring nip or autumn breeze. Remnants of upholstery fabrics are used for curtains and cushion covers, and the floor is wooden so sand can be swept up easily and the mats taken outside to shake clean. Wooden shelves provide a focus, holding collections of old mismatched plates. 'Treasures' collected from the beach – sand-polished glass, delicate shells and fishing-boat flotsam and jetsam – help to reinforce the hut's seaside feel, inside and out.

The enamel-topped table (with its handy drawer) and the gas cooker are not only practical but will also withstand the wear and tear of the harsh environment. When the beach hut is shut up for the night there's space for sun loungers and other items that have been taken outside for use during the day ◁

Above Paint is used to protect and preserve timber but the choice of colour plays an important part in the appearance and character of this hut.

Right and opposite Furnishings and decorations are a mix of vintage and second-hand finds from local shops and fairs, including a single iron bedstead, which acts as a sofa as well as a daybed.

Flip Down Beach House

New Zealand architect Ken Crosson wanted somewhere he and his family could enjoy down time close to nature and away from the speed and trappings of contemporary urban life.

Above and above right Panels that can be raised and lowered protect the house from the elements and provide security when the family aren't in residence.

Opposite Over time the cypress cladding has weathered to pale driftwood grey while inside hoop pine plywood walls, ceiling cladding and built-in units give a warmer, more yellow appearance. The contrast between the weathered 'cover' and the brighter interior 'pages' adds to the book-like impression of the construction.

Crosson's house is like a large book; when not in use its covers stay closed and secure against the elements, but when the family are in residence the front and back covers are lowered down by means of a motorized winch, to form platform decks and opening the house up to sunlight and sea breezes.

Fixtures and fittings have been kept deliberately simple; there is no dishwasher, television or computer so that the pace of life is slow and camp-style, with the majority of food preparation and cooking taking place outdoors.

The 120-square-metre (1,290-square-feet) house is built of thick planks of cypress over a frame of eucalyptus, whose slightly bitter aromatic smell scents the air in the warmth of a sunny day or when the log-burning stove is fired up on cool evenings.

Inside the wooden panels on the front and back elevations are glass bi-fold doors, which Crosson refers to as 'dissolving walls' because of their ability to disappear, but they add to the real connection between the building and the outdoors. There is also a bath on wheels that can be filled inside with hot soapy water and trundled out onto the deck for a soak under the night sky or to bask in the panoramic view of the white sandy beach and sea.

Although the house is a compact rectangle it has four bedrooms to accommodate family and friends, and each of the bathrooms have exterior doors that open to the outdoors so bathers can walk straight from the sea and into the shower without trailing sand through the main living area.

There is no clock watching when Crosson and his family come to their 'bach'; days are governed by the weather and daylight, and when they go back to the city, they simple close up the covers of their book-like house and keep their treasured memories safely shut up inside until the next visit ◁

Dutch Waterside Island Cabin

The cabin is much as it was when built in 1958 with tar-impregnated timber, an old insulating and preserving technique that was commonly used by farmers to protect their barns.

Above The tar-impregnated timber and whitewashed exterior of the island house. Tar or bitumen coating is no longer allowed in building, but in the past it acted as an effective waterproofing and timber preservative.

Left The newly built kitchen and bunk bed sleeping area in the redesigned interior.

Above This custom-built, adaptable seating area with pull out units can be rearranged to form beds for overnight visitors, with the deep cushions making comfortable mattresses. The log-burning stove provides heating for the main living and sleeping room.

Right, from left to right The chunky drawer and cupboard handles on the kitchen units echo those found on the pull-out beds. The outdoor dining and lounging space beside the house is used as another room during warm weather. Mature trees provide shade and a hanging place for a hammock. Chunky industrial chain and butcher's hooks have been made into hanging storage for kitchen equipment such as pans and coffee pots. A basic aluminium bucket is recycled as a basin.

Opposite, above The jetty is where the family tie up their boat when they have driven from their city home and sailed across the lake.

This small wooden house on an island in the Kaag lake region of the Netherlands is just 15 minutes drive, then a further 15 minutes by boat from the city centre home that Judith Spruijt and Arnold van der Molen share with their children Hidde and Dana. It's not far in travelling time but feels like a million miles away from their daily life near The Hague.

When the house was put on the market the previous owner was very particular about whom he would sell the place to, but Judith won him over with a personal letter about her childhood memories of water-focused family holidays with her parents and brother, her love of nature and of the location.

In this remote island location the surrounding vegetation had run wild and had to be severely cut back and controlled. The cabin was also devoid of power, fresh water and sewage facilities and it was a mammoth undertaking to connect the island to the mainland utilities, via underwater pipes and cables. Once these tasks were accomplished, and Spruijt and van der Molen had time to replenish their bank accounts, the interior of the cabin was tackled with the help of a friend, interior designer Jessica Bouvy. The cabin's 250-square-metre (2,690-square-feet) floor area was gutted, an internal wall and the kitchen were removed and a wood-burning stove installed in the centre of the now openplan living space. At one end is a sleeping area and at the other a sitting area. The kitchen was custom-made.

But the joy of the location is its remoteness and surrounding water. 'We all love the water and sail as often as we can. There is a sense of freedom here that suits us. It's not prim and proper, it's just our idea of paradise,' says Spruijt ◁

The Turtle House

Architects Maartje Lammers and Boris Zeisser of the Rotterdam-based practice 24H Architecture built this extraordinary summer home on the shore of Lake Övre Gla in southern Sweden's Glaskogen nature reserve.

Local building regulations limited the design by restricting the size to a proportion of the existing building, a cabin built in the late 1800s, and proximity to the site boundaries, which meant keeping beyond the 4-metre (13-feet) limit of the neighbouring stream and lake. Working within these guidelines they made an extension to the cabin that can 'literally adjust itself to its environment depending on the weather condition, season or number of occupants,' explains Maartje.

The pair devised a retractable 30-square-metre (323-square-foot) extension that can be rolled out using pulleys and a steel frame, but when not needed can be pulled in. 'The extension unfurls like a butterfly; during the winter it is a cocoon, with a double skin against the cold. During the summer it unfolds its wings. The cantilevered section projects out over the stream so one can sit above the water and listen to it murmur,' says Maartje.

The organic shape of the house helps it blend into the forest and its 'skin' of red cedarwood shingles, which naturally fades to grey, reflects the rocky outcrops. 'Traditional roofing tiles called *stickor* in Sweden were used in a contemporary way, but the local timber was too soft and would have required annual repainting, so we imported more durable cedar from Canada,' explains Boris.

Above and right The retractable 30-metre (100-foot) extension is clad with red cedar shingles. The extension spends part of the year under the covering of the main building, so has retained more of the original colour while the exterior has weathered to silvery grey.

Opposite A series of floor-to-ceiling windows open onto the stunning lake view.

Left Pillars of unstripped tree trunks support the overhang of the deck entrance to the house. The silver-grey bark of the pillars and the weathered deck wood and roof shingles help the extraordinary building to blend in with its woodland setting.

Right Reindeer hides are used to line the roof and walls of the building in winter, an idea taken from the local Sami people. A contemporary 'Birdie' ceiling light, designed by Ingo Maurer, makes an unusual reminder of the abundant wildlife outside.

Left The curving and undulating timber panelling gives the interior of the house a protective and cocoon-like quality, softening sounds and retaining the warmth; although the building materials are ancient the visual effect is modern and organic.

Below The furniture, like the gleaming wooden table, is simple and predominantly wooden, in keeping with this extraordinary building.

This extending wing of the house had no foundations and doesn't rest on the ground and, as with much of the commercial work they do through their practice, the form and shape is designed with the environment in mind. 'Closely following the biomorphic curves of the rib cage, the interior walls are finished with locally sourced pine lattice, and in the retractable extension they are covered with reindeer hides, turning the living area into a sensuous fur-lined cave. This idea came from the Sami people of northern Scandinavia and is an excellent form of insulation.

'There are only a few hours of darkness in the Swedish summertime but light fixtures were carefully chosen to blend with the natural surroundings. When you walk into the living area your footsteps cause the Ingo Maurer "Birdie" chandelier to flutter and in the kitchen and dining areas the red polycarbonate lights were inspired by the aurora borealis,' says Boris.

The environmental footprint of the house is small, it is almost CO_2 free, and cooking is by propane gas and heating by a wood-fuelled stove. The stream feeds the hot tub for bathing, lights are solar powered and the lavatory, in a hut at the end of a path, works without a septic tank. 'Houses normally only come alive in fairytales but this one really does. The fact that it tucks its head in when the temperature drops or that it hibernates under the snow in winter makes it all the more enchanting,' says Boris ◁

Dunton Springs
Colorado Cabins

When Christop Henkel came to Dunton in the Colorado Rockies in 1994 it was a ghost town set in a 80-hectare (200-acre) valley rimmed by the San Juan Mountain range with the river Dolores running through and extraordinary non-sulphurous natural hot springs near by.

The location is ideal for hiking, horse riding and fly fishing and in the winter cross-country skiing, but in its heyday Dunton was a hard-working mining town of 260 inhabitants. It thrived because of its proximity to the nearby Emma ore mine, but by 1918 it was derelict. It took German entrepreneur Henkel seven years to complete the work needed to restore and enhance the remaining viable buildings. The work involved taking each of the 12 cabins apart, putting down foundations and then rebuilding them using the original spruce logs and many of the traditional techniques. 'The white infill between the wood is called chinking,' explains Henkel's wife Katrin. 'It's a compound used to seal and keep the logs together. In the old days they made the filling with newspaper, but now a more robust and weatherproof, mortar-based product is used.'

During the rebuilding the cabins were adapted to accommodate modern amenities such as heating, bathrooms, hot water, telephone and internet, then Katrin, an art collector, and her childhood friend Annabelle Selldorf furnished the cabins with artefacts from Katrin's personal collection as well as adding comfortable classic sofas and armchairs.

Above **One of Dunton Springs' restored cabins with tipi in the shadow of the Colorado Rockies at dusk.**

Right **The wood-built Dolores cabin with its raised deck is now wired with electricity, providing light and hot water to the modern bathroom.**

Above The wood walls were traditionally made airtight using an infill of newspaper known as chinking; these days modern, breathable fillers do the job. The furnishings are an eclectic mix from Morocco, New Mexico, China and India, as though the previous owner of this home might have been a global traveller or trader.

In the Dolores cabin the unusually high wedding bed is from Rajasthan but was found by Katrin in an antique shop in Santa Fe, New Mexico. 'The details on the bed are amazing, and its base is skirted by little bells,' she says. 'We had the footstool made locally because it was difficult to clamber up on to the bed and I found the brilliant red bed cover and decorative curtains by the bathroom door while on a trip to Tibet. 'There is also an antique coat from southern China hanging on the wall and a large Moroccan carpet on the floor.

The outside retains its sense of more local history and feeling of the romance of this remote old mining town. The Dolores cabin sits just 3 metres (10 feet) from the river, which can be viewed at leisure from the covered deck. The sounds of the river provide a relaxing background tune while hummingbirds can be spotted among the lower tree branches and deer stroll by leisurely on their way for an evening drink ◁

Norwegian Wood

When sculptor Ian Garlant wants to get back to basics he heads north to a remote hut in a weather-beaten corner of southwest Norway.

Above and opposite In winter a bed is placed in the corner of the ground floor openplan living room, next to the stove. Built-in benches and handmade chairs are covered with woollen blankets, making them warm and comfortable.

Right The cabin is perched on the Hardanger Fjord.

Garlant explains: 'The place was built in 1940 as a boathouse but later became a refuge for my grandfather and his family. It was erected quickly and simply and survives only because it is tucked away in a small, sheltered cove on a tree-covered outcrop. Every year another patch of pitch and felt is added to seal a crack or leak. There's no running water and the day's events are invariably determined by the weather and the need to gather firewood and food, which is usually fish we catch. In summer we swim and watch the porpoises or walk through a landscape filled with wild flowers and apple blossom.' But Ian prefers the late autumn and winter when it is grey and moody. 'It's a land of contrasts,' he says, 'and a place where I can think and they do say that in every Norwegian there is an Ibsen.'

There are two bedrooms. The summer one is in the mellow wood-lined attic, with a single bed pushed up against the wall. Next door is the rudimentary bathroom, with a bowl resting on a small set of shelves and a tin 'dunny'. Ian's sparse collection of clothes hangs on the rails of a ladder at the top of the staircase. At the bottom of the staircase is the kitchen where a small oven supports an oversized kettle and dishes are washed when necessary in water transported by bucket. Food supplies are kept in tightly sealed tins and china containers, 'because,' Ian explains, 'the mice are also very hungry'.

Next to the kitchen is the cosy sitting room with a log-burning stove. By the one conventionally double-glazed window there is a desk and an easel where Ian paints and looks out over the waters of the fjord. In a corner is a chest of drawers with an old valve radio and a wall-hung oil lamp. 'It's a romantic place though not sentimental,' says Ian. 'The house has many family connections but I don't dwell on them, although I have kept the wooden clogs as a reminder of how hard life was for my grandfather and his contemporaries' ◁

Beach House in the Dunes

A light and airy beach house set among sandy dunes has been restored and then adapted several times to make the most of its stunning Suffolk beachside location.

Above The upper level 'sundowner' terrace was added to enjoy evening drinks with river and marshland views.

Right From the ground-floor living room the afternoon eyrie on the mezzanine area is visible above the kitchen.

Above The afternoon seating area is positioned on the mezzanine above the kitchen, viewed from the morning coffee space on the opposite mezzanine.

Left The rear elevation of the house incorporates the sundowner terrace on the left and the glass-sided dormer window on the right.

Opposite, above Contemporary artwork and furniture make a feature of the front porch.

Opposite, below The view of sand dunes and the seashore is framed by the window of the mezzanine afternoon sitting area. The comfortable built-in seats have adjustable panels that can be raised to make sloping back supports for lounging and reading.

Twenty-five years ago jewellery designer and gallery owner Lesley Craze went to Suffolk on a caravan trip with a friend, and fell in love with the place. 'Soon after that trip I bought "The Hutch" a tiny, wooden-clad dwelling. It didn't have a bathroom or kitchen but a local builder helped me make it sound and habitable. But soon I wanted to stay for longer periods and needed more space for myself and my two children, so I put letters through all my neighbours' doors saying that if they wanted to sell to let me know. Nothing happened for ages, then the phone rang and the owner of this property said he was interested in selling. After some negotiation I bought the place and again, with the help of the local builder, we started from scratch.'

The project has been ongoing. 'I didn't employ an architect, the scheme just evolved. I, John Briggs the builder, and more recently his son Jonathan would suggest something and if we thought it would work we did it. For example, a dormer window was being built and through a rip in the protective sheeting I saw the moon. I told John and instead of solid side panels he made them of glass.

'A year ago I thought it would be nice to have a terrace at the back, somewhere to enjoy the evening light and watch boats sailing along the river. We had a discussion and Jonathan relocated a water tank and made the terrace; he also put in a new staircase and opened up the ceiling into the beams.'

The furnishings of Craze's custom-made home also reflects its location. The front of the chalet-style building faces the sea; dunes topped with wiry grasses and on the horizon, the Dutch coast. So the southeast-facing breakfast terrace, afternoon eyrie and her grandchildren's bedroom are decorated in blue and white. At the back, which overlooks marshland and the river Blythe, the sun downer terrace and conservatory dining room are in schemes of green and white.

Craze also has the work of contemporary designers and artists in her home. 'There are good inspiring galleries locally and I have boought artwork from them.' Craze is also a fan of the local farmer's market and is up early to get to the stalls before the crush, walking along the dune-top path at an energetic pace ◁

The Tin House

This metal building was the sole and derelict remnant of a 1920s affordable house scheme when Robert Lance Hughes acquired it.

Below **The Tin House 'rests lightly on the earth' in a wildflower meadow beside a freshwater pond.**

Opposite, above **Double doors on adjacent walls of the sitting room open onto a panoramic view of the countryside.**

Opposite, below **A new deck was added to the back of the house.**

Lance Hughes explains the history of the building: 'It had been a family home for many years but latterly was stabling for a horse – horseshoe indentations in the panelling and teeth marks on some of the wood can still be seen.' On close inspection Lance Hughes noticed that some of the metal wall panels were corroded. 'I found a local corrugated roofing specialist, Thomas of Pencombe near Leominster, and took bits of the rusting sheeting to their offices. People came from all over the building to see it because of its unusual configuration,' he says.

When it came to doing up the Tin House, Lance Hughes took inspiration from the work of Australian-based architect Glenn Murcutt. 'Murcutt's philosophy to "live simply and in harmony with nature" came from his childhood in New Guinea and he is also fond of quoting the Aboriginal proverb "Touch the earth lightly"'. So with these ideas in mind Lance Hughes set about consolidating and renovating. To the back of the building he added a veranda raised on legs so that it appears to hover above the ground. The renovated roof is a butterfly design that

is lower in the centre and raised at the front and back. 'The house was bright blue but we painted over that with red oxide hoping that in time the red will peel and reveal some of the blue beneath, giving it a mottled, aged appearance which will sit better in the landscape. I wanted to maintain the deception of the building being a shed from the outside, but needed to make the inside comfortable and to maximize the limited space,' says Lance Hughes. He achieved this by accentuating the long view across the back of the house with a single long corridor and three new pairs of glass doors opening on to the veranda.

A galley-style kitchen is incorporated as part of the corridor, as is the doorway to the separate lavatory and hand basin. In the bedroom, in what looks like a cupboard, is a walk-in shower. The spacious living room has windows on three sides looking over the surrounding marshland as well as a skylight. 'The place is furnished with cast-offs and hand me downs,' says Lance Hughes, and the well-worn Welsh blankets and mismatched plates add to the relaxed and magical atmosphere of the place ◁

Left The tongue and groove panelled bedroom is heated both by the log-burning stove next door and its metal flue, which winds its way through the adjoining wall.

Below left A galley kitchen runs along one side of the internal corridor at the back of the house.

This page Books to be browsed on rainy days are ranged along a single shelf, while the log-burning stove is set on a slate plinth to protect the wooden floor

Australian Tower Shack

This weather-beaten copper-clad tower, perched high up on a mountain top in New South Wales, must be the ultimate bush escape.

Above The only way to get to the house is on foot or by horse, which helps to preserve the remoteness and unspoilt nature of the location.

Above right A shower consisting of a water bag suspended from a tree branch provides a fresh and exhilarating start to the day.

Opposite A water tank, made from the same metal as the house, collects and stores rain from the roof.

It is so isolated there are no signs of human habitation anywhere on the 800-hectare (1,975-acres)site. 'The landscape is rugged with granite boulders, dead ring-barked trees, stunted gums and wispy grasses and it is where, as a child, the client used to ride his horse and camp out. His desire to preserve this remoteness means that the tower is only approached by horse,' says the tower's architect Rob Brown of Casey Brown Architecture.

The tower is small, just 3 by 3 metres (10 x 10 feet) and 6 metres (20 feet) high. 'One step up from camping but able to resist the elements,' says Brown. 'It is used only occasionally, but has a two-layer, highly insulated facade, making it easy to warm quickly when there is snow on the ground, but also situated high enough up the hill to remain cool even in summer.'

Brown devised the tower so that the corrugated copper sides lift up like awnings and reveal the warm, oiled timber interior. During the day the awnings become raised canopies, providing valuable shade and protecting the house and its inhabitants from the harsh sun. But when it's time to pack up and leave the house these sides, operated by nautical winches, fold down, protecting the interior from the ravages of the harsh elements and wild animals.

Within the ironbark timber frame Brown created two levels, with a basic living area on the ground and a bed in the upper loft space, reached by ladder. 'It feels as though you're sleeping in a treehouse and being higher up does give a sense of security in the bush,' says Brown.

Opposite Glass louvre panels can be angled to allow cooling breezes to enter the house, but also closed to protect against sandstorms and insects.

Above The living space has a small shelf area for food preparation, a large log-burning stove as a heat source and floor cushions and mats for lounging.

Above right A basic ladder leads up to the timber-clad sleeping area, simply furnished with a mattress, blanket and oil lantern light.

The legs of the building are made of steel to protect against the ravages of white ants and to be resistant to bush fires. On the roof a tank collects and stores rainwater and dispenses it by gravity to a sink inside. The place is off-grid, so light is provided by oil lamps, and a wood-burning stove is the main source of heat.

A separate 'long-drop' toilet tower was erected a 'short hop and a skip around the gum trees'. This utility tower is a smaller replica of the main structure and was built first to test the mortice and tenon construction, originally favoured by Chinese craftsmen. Because of its remote location, without running water, electricity or roads to get the machinery there, no builder was prepared to work on site, so the buildings were prefabricated in a more hospitable location, then dismantled and reassembled on their final, remote site ◁

The Silo

This reimagining of an agricultural grain store on a farm in Wales as a comfortable and relaxing home is the ultimate sustainable and environmentally friendly development.

When Robert Lance Hughes bought Cwmhir Court, just inside the Welsh border near Hay-on-Wye, it came complete with a Norman arch, monastic heritage and breathtaking views of the nearby Black Mountains. 'When this place was a working arable farm there were a number of silos for storing grain,' he says, and for Lance Hughes, who studied at the Architectural Association, it was the round silos that grabbed his attention with their potential.

In the late 1980s while on a trip to Russia he became interested in the work of the Constructivist artist and architect Konstantin Melnikov. 'Melnikov's own home was round and although I couldn't bring the house back I had always thought that one day I would make my own interpretation of it, transporting the dream.' And the silos seemed to offer an opportunity to fulfil that dream.

'The silo is light and sturdy but you can't cut into the rounded walls without compromising the structural strength, so we built an internal wooden frame before cutting in to make the doors and windows,' he explains. 'We also insulated between the corrugated skin and wooden frame with the type

Above and right Panels of corrugated metal removed when the windows were installed have been reused as shutters.

Opposite The Silo is located on the edge of a farm with uninterrupted views of the Black Mountains.

of quilted tinfoil that is used in the construction of space shuttles.' Then, with the help of local craftsmen, plasterboard walls were added. 'We dampened and gently bent the plasterboard until it curved and then let it dry in situ. In fact, we made up a lot of the construction processes as we went along,' he admits, and it took almost five months to complete the conversion.

'Once we put in the internal floor and divided the space into two levels, we made segment-like sections to create the ground floor rooms.' These consist of a double bedroom, separate lavatory, well-equipped galley kitchen and walk-in shower room. A curving white-washed red cedar staircase winds up to the simply furnished living space, where three strategically placed windows provide an uninterrupted view of sheep-speckled fields.

'As part of the conservation of the building I left the original openings as windows, so where the grain was pumped in and out there are now small square windows. Where we cut new openings we used the surplus metal to make shutters so that when the silo isn't being used they can be closed over and it looks just as it was' ◁

Above Two of the three floor-to-ceiling windows give the first floor living area clear views of Welsh countryside and the changing weather.

Opposite, above Although the Silo is an old farm building the modern, minimal interior is perfectly suited to contemporary furniture.

Right The staircase to the upper floor curves to follow round the circular outer wall of the silo.

Far right Vintage Welsh woollen blankets and throws bring a touch of local craft and comfort to the bedroom. Even from bed you can enjoy the fresh air and views.

stone & clay

Opposite *Locally sourced, roughly hewn rock and rubble stones have long been used to build walls and dwellings; here the structure has been bonded together with simple mortar.* **Above** *Cave dwellings have been used since historic times and may still be found in use in warmer climates, where the cavernous spaces are cool and give shelter from the intense heat of the sun.*

Bothies and cottages are usually constructed from locally available stone, because it is a heavy and costly material to transport. The type of stone in that area may also dictate the construction of the building – for example, softer, laterally grained stone such as slate is often used in thin overlapping layers, like wooden shingles, as cladding or roof tiles, while rounded shapes in hard rock such as granite can be assembled in a dry-wall configuration.

Dry-stone walling is a building method using stones without mortar or a binding agent to cement them in place. The structures are stable because of the careful selection and alignment of interlocking stones, which are put together like a jigsaw.

Some stone walls are straight, forming square or rectangular buildings, while others are curved, such as those found in the Italian *trullo*, which is built like an igloo, with larger blocks or stones at the base, tapering up to smaller, flatter ones on the roof. Many stone buildings started life as a temporary field shelter or store and were later transformed into simple homes.

Dry-stone wall construction is seen widely across the Mediterranean, north of England, Scotland and West of Ireland. Settlers from these areas are thought to have taken the technique with them to Canada, New South Wales and the United States where it is found in areas of rocky ground such as New England, Pennsylvania, central Kentucky and northern California.

Stone-built houses are resilient and hard-wearing and will withstand the elements. Thick stone walls ensure these house are cool indoors in summer and warm in winter and would originally have had just one or two small windows because glass was an expensive luxury. In many modern conversions sky or roof lights are added to bring more natural light to the interior.

Some stone-built houses actually incorporate the face of a hill or rocky outcrop into their construction, saving on the material and labour needed for the building of a fourth wall. The existing natural feature would also provide a stable face onto which the other walls could be attached. A rocky outcrop may in itself provide a dwelling, for example the cave houses of Göreme in Turkey's Cappadocia region and the historic homes in Walnut Canyon, Flagstaff, Arizona.

Mud is also a natural and versatile building material that can be applied over a wooden and wicker frame and built up in layers or shaped into bricks. Adobe is a style of mud-brick building seen in the warm, dry areas of New Mexico and Arizona. Sand, clay and straw are mixed and packed into moulds or shaped by hand then left for about a month to dry in the sun. The bricks can then be used to build a structure that is mortared together with fresh, wet adobe.

In parts of the United Kingdom, Africa and Afghanistan some of the oldest man-made structures are built from cob, which like adobe is made from a mixture of sand, clay, water and straw. Because of its organic and sustainable nature, cob is going through a revival.

Opposite, clockwise from top left *This two-storey, lakeside boathouse has room to store a vessel and equipment at the lower level with accommodation on the upper floor, which has an uninterrupted view of the water and surrounding shore. This cave-like dwelling has walls finished with a light clay render that have been painted white to enhance the feeling of light and space. An old stone-built house has a roof finished with finely cut slate tiles, the weight of which can be supported by the solid walls. Exposed stone walls and large paving slabs complement the roughly hewn beams and wooden cupboard doors.*

Stone cabins

Rock is one of the strongest and most enduring building materials and has provided shelter and homes through the centuries. Early man found refuge in naturally formed rock caves before venturing out to build his own simple stone dwellings. These were made using locally found rubble rocks piled one on top of another and topped off with a reed or straw roof. This simple, low-tech dry-wall building technique used by early man is still found in dwellings today.

The type of rock available in an area will dictate the colour and style of a vernacular building – for example, the so-called 'soft' sedimentary rocks such as limestone and sandstone come in mellow colours in the spectrum of ochre, beige, taupe and, in some cases, lavender pink and greyish hues. These stones are relatively easy to carve and cut so can be used in more decorative and structured designs. They can also be machine cut into brick-like blocks and cemented together with mortar.

Igneous rock such as granite is hard and brittle and infused with sparkling elements of quartz and mica. These materials are hard and difficult to cut accurately by hand, but flint stones can be used in dry-stone walling or embedded into mortar as a weatherproof cladding or facing to a building. Metamorphic rock is a sedimentary or igneous rock that has been changed under intense heat or pressure. Marble, slate and alabaster are all metamorphic and generally need to be quarried, mined or artificially extracted making them expensive, so unlikely to be used in quantities in a simple building, although reclaimed or recycled stone may be more affordable.

Where mortar has not been used in the construction of a stone building there may be small gaps in the walls, traditionally packed with lichen or moss. In time some of this natural material would, on the outer face of the walls, become damp with rain and dew and continue to grow, giving older houses a mossy covering that made them blend into their surroundings.

Opposite *Slabs of rock were traditionally used to build dry-stone walls. The technique does not require mortar because the stones are skilfully arranged and laid to overlap, their weight anchoring and stabilizing the wall.* **Above right** *Although built in 1999 Bodrifty Roundhouse was constructed using the same techniques and materials as Celtic Iron Age builders employed when they erected conical thatched and low granite-wall dwellings.* **Right** *In ancient times fires were smoky log piles on an earth hearth in the centre of the room, but with the development of chimneys the smoke could be ducted away.*

Above *The clay walls of this single-storey house have been whitewashed to give a crisp, clean appearance. In some countries the whitewash is reapplied annually and is often connected to a feast day.* **Above centre** *Lighthouses are cylindrical because the rounded shape helps to reduce the effect of wind on a tall building. Many lighthouses have been sold as their function has been replaced by satellite navigation and automated warning systems.* **Above right** *A 'home from home' as temporary escape from reality has led to some unusual and interesting constructions known as follies. A folly is built for fun and pleasure and is often a miniature or scaled down version of a grander building, such as a castle or tower.*

Clay and brick

Clay is a fine-grained, often mineral-rich soil, found around the banks and shorelines of large lakes, rivers and seas. Marine deposits are often very fine and come into the category of silt, whereas it is the larger grain varieties that are used in building and the making of ceramics. As well as being an ancient material used in the fabrication of dwellings it is estimated that clay has been used in the construction of buildings where one half of the world's population live or work today.

Clay is a natural and versatile substance and widely used in eco and traditional construction techniques, such as cob, adobe

and rammed earth, as well as finishes such as wattle and daub, plaster, render, floors and paints. Clay can be applied to a frame of thin, interwoven branches or slats fixed between upright stakes. When mixed with reinforcing agents, such as chalk or limestone dust and fillers such as hay or straw, which provide flexibility and help control shrinkage, clay is referred to as daub.

The daub may be mixed by hand or by treading and applied to the wicker or wood frame and allowed to dry. Sometimes a layer of paint such as limewash or whitewash (always natural rather than synthetic to allow the clay to breathe) will be applied. In some cases this is to increase the clay's resistance to rain and othr elements, and in others it is for mainly decorative reasons or as a symbol of tribal unity.

In some countries the plaster finish is painted in solid, bright shades or with intricate designs; for example the huts and houses of the Xhosa people of South Africa stand out against the dry, dusty earth of the landscape because of their brilliant colours, which include pink, lilac and turquoise green, and the Ndebele decorate the exterior of their homes with intricate geometric patterns that are similar in style to some of the Ikat patterns of India and Aztec motifs found in South America.

In parts of Africa homes are often made up from a collection of single-room huts, one for cooking, another for meeting and separate ones for sleeping; by painting the exterior of the huts in a single bright colour it is easy to identify and recognize which huts make up a family unit.

Opposite *When sun-baked and dried to a firm surface, clay walls can be painted in a range of colours. In hot countries white is popular because it reflects sunlight and keeps the inside of the building cool, whereas in other places earth colours and natural pigments are prevalent.*

Right *In keeping with the clay-based structure of this building an eco-friendly grass and sedum roof has been installed. The plants are bedded on a waterproof membrane and their foliage and leaf matter will not only absorb the water but also provide insulation.*

The main problem with a clay-built home is that it will need regular and careful maintenance, and in time the clay may have to be hacked off and replaced. This is especially prevalent in hot countries where, over years, the clay will dry out and become brittle, then crack and flake.

If building a clay or cob home from scratch it is important to ensure that the foundations are dry and sturdy so that even after torrential rain the base of the building will not be standing in water. Clay is absorbent and any residual water will permeate and cause the clay to become soft and loose. A pitched, over-hanging roof is another good way of protecting clay walls as the angle and projectory of the roof will allow water or snow to run off well away from the walls.

If a clay wall does become damaged it is relatively simple to repair. The broken or dented area can be raked out and smoothed down, then another layer of clay plaster applied, levelled and left to dry. In time it will blend in and be almost indistinguishable from the rest of the wall.

Bricks are also made from clay. Some, such as those used in adobe buildings, are hand-formed and baked dry in the sun while more durable types are shaped in moulds, giving them uniform, regular shapes, kiln fired to a hard ceramic finish, then laid in regular rows and joined by mortar. Bricks are believed to be one of the longest-lasting and strongest man-made building materials used throughout history since Roman times.

When, in the eighteenth century, the factory production of bricks was established, their availability increased and the price also came down, so they became more widely used and rapidly replaced stone as the major building material. During the nineteenth-century building boom in New York and Boston many brick and timber houses were constructed, initially for the emerging middle class property owners, but in time for more modest cottages and rural dwellings.

Bricks come in a variety of colours such as red, grey and beige; these can be used to create decorative patterns within the structure or to highlight a feature such as a doorway or window. Brick-built structures may be given a smooth seal of plaster or dilute clay, which will give a softer more refined finish, which in turn may be painted or colour washed. The smooth surface can also be used as a canvas for decorative painting, such as murals or motifs and faux architraves around windows and doorways, which give the illusion of a more expensive and detailed finish.

Living

The living spaces in clay, brick and stone-built homes tend to be sturdy, warm and well insulated; the raw building material can be left natural and exposed, or some of the walls can be plastered, painted or clad with wood panelling or tongue and groove, leaving a single wall, or area of wall, as a feature.

It is quite common to find that a prominent part of a living area, such as a fireplace or window seat surround or sill, is left exposed so that they eye is drawn to it when entering the room. Sometimes a group of just a few stones or bricks are left uncovered; again, this gives a reference to the actual fabric and character of the building, preventing the area from looking too finished and bland, which would be inappropriate in a simple and casual style of dwelling.

In rooms with few or small windows it can be advantageous to plaster and paint the walls; many natural materials such as stone are dark and absorb light, whereas smooth, white-painted walls will reflect it and make the room appear brighter and lighter. But avoid making the plaster too smooth and polished – a little texture and even streaky, water-wash-style painting can add to the carefree look of the place. When you choose a brick or stone cabin as a hideaway from home you want to enjoy its rustic charm not disguise it.

Opposite *A fine clay screed has been applied to these walls. This finish allows the rustic stonework to show through and reveal its rough-hewn character while providing a seal against loose bits of stone and grit.* **Right** *A more conventional clay plaster has been used to conceal the construction of these walls and provide a smooth, rounded finish.*

Eating

Below *Clay surfaces are absorbent so it may be necessary to seal and protect them to prevent staining by oil and grease.* **Below right** *Bare brick work can be an attractive feature but it should be kept well away from direct contact with food preparation because it is difficult to wash and keep the brick clean.* **Right** *This wall built of irregular blocks of stone has been given a uniform appearance by being painted white.* **Opposite, below left** *This kitchen wall is finished with a smooth plaster while the original brickwork has been left exposed as a feature in the arch.* **Opposite, below right** *Plain plaster walls can be whitewashed regularly to maintain their clean appearance.*

Kitchen and dining spaces should be easy to keep clean and hygienic, so it is often through necessity that areas of exposed walls have to be plastered or tiled. It can be laborious to even out stone and brick walls to support tiling and those made of clay may not be strong enough, but in cases such as these a freestanding back board maybe the solution.

The board can be secured to the back of the draining board and sink unit surround rather than to the wall. Brackets or strut supports attached to the back of the board and then to the units will make it firm and secure. Once it is in place tiles or vinyl paint, stain or varnish can be applied to make the splashback waterproof. Instead of choosing a uniform panel of matching tiles you could try a colour-themed mix-and-match collection of plain and patterned vintage ones.

Food, utensil and tableware storage may also be tricky, because if the location has uneven walls and floors it will be difficult to fit standard kitchen units. But a mix of freestanding dressers, vintage cabinets and small tables can create not

only ample storage and work area but also an interesting and individual look that sits better in an unsophisticated building.

With an uneven floor it is easier to level out the legs of an individual cabinet or cupboard, simply by adding a wedge of wood or a door jamb under a leg. With fitted units the run of cupboards have to be level, otherwise they look odd to the eye and the lack of level may cause the worktop to crack or break.

You may also choose to create storage that alludes to your location. For example, for a cliffside cabin well-scrubbed wooden fish boxes or driftwood could be used as shelves; in a rural area baskets and wicker hampers can be used for fruit and vegetable storage; and elsewhere old trunks make useful linen stores and wine boxes can be recycled as drawers.

Often the floor area of a cabin is small and space is at a premium, so instead of cupboards and units with opening doors you could use curtains or sliding doors that don't require an area in front to open, and for things that are in regular daily use, open shelves and dressers may be the best option.

Sleeping

It is best if possible to keep the bed away from direct contact with rough and exposed wall surfaces, because you may graze your skin if you rub or bump up against it, bed linen could became soiled or damaged and it will also be cold and uncomfortable to touch. A headboard or iron bedstead will create a barrier between your head and pillows and the wall, or you could try a fabric wall hanging or rug to create a barrier.

It can be difficult to hang pictures and artefacts on uneven wall surfaces, and stone and brick can be tricky to get a hook or nail into, so colourful bed throws, cushions and curtains can help to bring personality to a space. A Pendleton geometric-patterned Native American blanket manufactured by the Pendleton Company or a Hudson Bay Point blanket of cream

wool with red, yellow and green stripes, once traded for fur pelts, have history and interest. These woollen wall hangings will also help to insulate and soften the sound in the room.

Stone walls may be a blessing during hot weather because the room will be cool and shady, making it easier to sleep, but in winter they may make the space very cold so you will need a fire or extra thick duvet, eiderdown or blanket and a hot-water bottle. Shutters or thick, well-lined curtains will also help to insulate and retain the heat once you have got the room warm.

Opposite *The wall against which this bed is placed has been plastered to a smooth and level finish, which means that the bed can be placed directly against it without the need for a headboard or other layer.* **Right** *In a small or windowless room a straightforward wash of light-coloured paint will prevent the space from feeling claustrophobic and give it a fresh and attractive appearance* **Far right** *Clay is absorbent and needs to 'breathe' so never paint cob or clay walls with oil-based or latex products and avoid filling or repairing with cement.* **Below right** *Exposed stone in a variety of natural hues forms a textural backdrop to modern art. The stone wall should be brushed several times with a wire brush and then with a smooth bristle brush or paintbrush to remove any loose stone or grit.*

Swiss Mountain Chalet

Perfectly settled in its Alpine setting this stone-built lodge combines modern conveniences with traditional architecture.

Antwerp-based collector, designer and dealer Axel Vervoordt wrote a list on the back of an envelope and gave it to his sons Boris and Dick. It itemized the things that he was looking for in a location and property that would become their family retreat. The list read:

in a French-speaking area
near water
south-facing with winter snow but without a ski lift in sight
perhaps an old local house such as a *mazot*
drivable from the family's main home in Belgium

Vervoordt's sons spent the best part of a year looking for somewhere that fulfilled their father's criteria but couldn't. Their searches were fruitless, but rather than admit defeat or compromise on his requirements Vervoordt decided to start from scratch. He found and bought the right location, on a hilltop near Verbier, and built a new 'old' house from scratch.

The description 'old' new house is because although the building looks as though it has stood on the mountain top for centuries, it is in fact a new build using recycled, locally sourced wood and stone and, with the help of architects Marcel Fellay and Raymond Bruchez, constructed in the vernacular style of a Valasian farmhouse.

Above and top right Locally sourced recycled stone was brought to the mountain-side location to build this new but traditional-style chalet.

Right and far right A sheltered area under the extended roof provides a perfect casual dining area with unhindered views of the magnificent scenery.

Not only were well-aged materials used, but to ensure the authentic look of the building, local craftsmen were employed to use traditional construction methods, such as pegging the wooden beams rather than nailing and pulley mechanisms for opening and closing the shutters.

Behind the ancient-looking stone and wood walls the house is the epitome of comfort and style but with the emphasis very much on simplicity. Modern conveniences are discreetly concealed to maintain the rustic feel of the place. There is underfloor heating and a hammam. The garage and wood store are under the house so that cars and unnecessary clutter can be hidden from view and not detract from the uninterrupted mountain views.

The location gives the house a still and serene quality and the wood-lined interiors add to the warm and protective ambience. Curtains are of unlined natural linen and the floors are only occasionally covered, and then with simple strips of wool felt. In one of the bedrooms is a pair of cosy built-in box beds, in another a basic wood -frame bed.

'The simple furniture is a reminder of how little we need to achieve comfort,' says Vervoordt ◁

Right Ski boots and outdoor
gear can be hung up and dried
in the stone-floored boot room;
each member of the family has
a named basket in which to
store their socks, scarves, hats
and mittens.

Above Muted paint colours and traditional carved panel box beds add to the illusion that this chalet has been on the mountain side for generations. Simple red-and-white gingham bed linen adds a splash of colour to the otherwise wood-dominated interior.

Above right The decorative lightwood furniture is both beautiful and useful. Cupboards and armoires are used to store linens as well as clothing and in the kitchen also contain foodstuffs.

Right With breathtaking mountain scenery and a constantly changing range of weather to observe, little more than a good range of windows is needed to decorate this room.

Snug in a Bothy

'Bothy' derives from the Gaelic word *bothan*, the Welsh *bwthy* and Norse *bûð*, referring to a basic shelter, usually left unlocked and available for anyone to use free of charge.

This stone bothy in northeast Scotland was once used by shepherds supervising their flocks; now it is the holiday home of artist and carpet designer Catriona Stewart, whose family once owned a large estate in the area. The bothy is located on rough pasture between a sea loch and a hill loch; there is no road so once the path peters out you have to scramble over the rocky shoreline or row a boat to get there. Catriona made a coracle (a traditional round, lightweight canvas-and-wood boat), which is easy to carry and which she uses for travelling or fishing.

Catriona and her family modified this bothy to create a bedroom on an upper floor. The low, sloping eaves of the roof, though, allow space only for mattresses on the floor –no four-poster bed possibilities here. The walls are constructed from thick stones so it was difficult to put up hooks and screws. Catriona devised a way of attaching sturdy wires around the lumps of rock and then securing them to the fish boxes she uses as shelves.

Even when the days are warm the nights can be bitterly cold with chilly winds blowing across the sea loch, so the log-burning stove, thick wool rugs of Catriona's design and tartan blankets are essential, but also add to the colour and cosiness of the place ◁

Above There isn't a lot of room indoors so when friends come by picnics are the answer. Freshly caught prawns and fish are enjoyed during the summer months caught from Catriona's coracle, seen propped up by the bothy door.

Above centre Adding the upper floor provided wooden beams to which hooks for the frequently used hot-water bottles can be attached.

Above right The wood-burning stove was made from discarded bits of pipe and car parts by a local blacksmith.

Opposite The attic bedroom is light from dawn as the sun rises and shines through the Perspex roof panels. Head height is restricted so mattresses are placed on the floor.

Italian Island Cave

Hewn out of the cliffs above a bustling Italian harbour, this home is inspiring in its truly elemental construction, and warm and organic in its styling.

Marina Klemente was born in Irpinia in southern Italy and began her career in Rome as a set and graphic designer. Although her work required her to be city based she did not really enjoy urban living, so decided to explore a different lifestyle. This search took her to Filicudi on one of the Aeolian islands northeast of Sicily.

While holidaying there Marina met a man who had made himself a home in a cave, and having visited his unusual dwelling she decided to do the same. After some searching, Marina managed to buy an old cave high up on a hill overlooking the main port and a promontory called Capo Graziano, and with the help of a few friends, began to dig herself a home.

She has now lived there for almost 20 years and in a series of natural caves has established home and studio. The roughly hewn bare rock is limewashed, giving it a fresh white and airy appearance, and the various niches, natural openings and platforms provide her with a bedroom, living room with skylight, kitchen and bathroom, as well as a series of outdoor terraces. The structure is also biodynamic, with its own drinking water and drainage system and recycled water system.

Above The sea view from one of the cave's eyrie-like terraces is stunning.

Right and opposite Conventional double doors lead from the cave rooms to a sunny terrace. From inside the cave they frame the magnificent view of the harbour and town below.

Left The main sleeping area is on an elevated platform of rock, and by placing the mattress on the floor rather than a bedstead there is adequate head height. White-painted walls and a small window give this internal space a clean and bright appearance.

Above A semi-circular hood directs smoke from the fire up though a hole in the cave roof so preventing the room from becoming smoky. A couple of rocks peeping through the smooth clay floor provide a spark-resistant hearth.

'It may be hard for some people to imagine living in a cave,' she says, 'but for me it's the best place, and I feel that it is good for both my body and soul.'

The location also provides Marina with inspiration and a source of materials for her design work. When strolling along the nearby beaches she picks up bits of flotsam and jetsam, battered by the sea and weathered by the sun, and these she transforms into sculptures and light fittings, some of which find their way into her unusual home, while others are sold through local galleries and shops.

Although the structure is hard and unforgiving, Marina has managed to make it a comfortable and easy place to be – various rugs bring colour and softness to the floor, and openings, whether windows or doors, allow plenty of natural light and air to circulate, so avoiding the feeling of being hemmed in. The thick walls also provide natural insulation, keeping the cavern-like rooms warm and secure in winter, but cool and shady in the heat of high summer. But best of all are the views, uninterrupted and constantly changing vistas of the sea and sky ◁

South African Rondavel

Secluded in a forested garden and yet close to the city, taking the best of local architectural traditions and giving them a modern spin, this thatched home combines the best of all worlds.

South African architects Silvio Rech and Lesley Carstens use local craftsmanship and know-how in their award-winning 'designs based on nature' and this can be seen in their own home, built in the heart of a forested indigenous garden in Westcliff Ridge, Johannesburg.

Rech and Carstens were attracted by the wildness of the area and started constructing their home in 1998. 'At the time we were using it as a base to return to from our travels, but we now live here permanently with our two children and have moved our architectural practice here as well,' says Carstens.

The house follows traditional Highveld design with the kitchen and various rooms as outbuildings, rather than one large house. The construction of the rondavels (round buildings) uses primitive techniques and materials such as thatch, stone and mud, with pigmented screed floors and thick walls to protect against the intense African heat. But this natural and primitive style of building requires regular maintenance, with new thatch for the roof and patching for damaged walls.

Above Traditional thatch, stone and mud has been used in the construction.

Above and opposite The table, benches and the light fitting, made from flexible acrylic hosepipe, were all designed by Rech and Carstens.

Oposite The altar-like bed is raised off the floor on a 2-metre (7-foot) high stepped mud plinth. There is a space underneath for a child's bed, which Carsten says is 'like a baby sleeping in the belly of the forest'. A basic wooden ladder is used to climb up onto the bed and a cotton canopy prevents loose thatch from dropping onto the mattress.

Above Bench seats, built around the curved rondavel walls, provide ample seating while allowing the centre of the space to be used for an oversized bed construction. A shelf for displaying some of the couples collection of objects gathered on their travels has also been built into the wall.

Above right The basin was carved from a chunk of volcanic Balinese rock and the walls have been reinforced with a textured paint, which bonds with the mud while allowing its surface texture to show.

'We have mains supply electricity, water and sewage and in some places we have added cement and textured cementitous paint to make the walls more resilient. During the rains the water damage to the basic mud walls can be quite severe,' explains Carsten. But she adds, 'The traditional building style and materials gives the space a special mellow colouration and soothing quality; our home is a calm oasis against the frenetic pace of city life.'

There is a strong traditional element to the buildings, but the furnishings have contemporary influences. 'We design new pieces of furniture for various projects, we also collect African sculpture and pick up things when we travel in the East and Europe.' The mix is eclectic; the stone basin in the bathroom is carved from volcanic rock found in Bali, while the mirror frame is modern steel and the hanging cutouts above the bed are taken from templates of plants in the garden. 'Although we live in the heart of Johannesburg the garden is full of life. Frogs and crickets chatter through the night and we have a large bird and butterfly population,' says Carstens of her indigenous-inspired home ◁

treehouses

Opposite *This traditional style of thatched treehouse is popular in Africa. Being raised above the ground it takes advantage of cool air and shade found among the tree canopy while also being at a safe distance from wild animals.* **Above** *Contemporary treehouse design offers many interesting and unusual choices; this box appears to be hanging in mid-air while access is by a series of rope-hung walkways.*

Shelters raised above the ground would protect their inhabitants from wild animals, marauding enemy tribes and flood waters, but now the aspect most sought after is the closeness to a canopy of leaves and abundant fresh air. Although often thought of as a play area for children, treehouses are increasingly becoming a grown-up domain, with larger platform bases and more sophisticated construction making it possibly to live in them for longer periods.

The joy of a treehouse is that it brings you close to nature. You can see crisp new leaves unfurl in front of you, watch them mature and grow, then change colour and fall so that the view from your tree-high window is constantly changing. Being above ground level also means that the wind can be a regular companion, whistling through leaves and shaking the branches – you may also get panoramic views of the surrounding countryside as well as the moon and stars at night.

There are various eco and environmental aspects to modern treehouse construction and many are designed to make minimal use of nails and screws or any type of fixing that might affect the tree. Some trees are more susceptible to puncture damage, which can lead to sap leakage and bark peeling. Many architects and designers working on treehouse construction use specially developed attachments known as anchor bolts or TAB.

There is also a growing trend for prefabricated pods to be built off-site and then hoisted into the tree, to be set nest-like among the branches and then secured in place. The ecological advantage of this type of controlled construction is that all the materials can be assembled and used within the regulated environment of a workshop of factory. It then requires only one lorry or transporter to bring the finished house to site, rather than repeated visits by various vans and contractors.

Once the treehouse is in situ access needs to be installed. This can be by a simple wooden staircase or ladder, or for those who feel fit and able a rope ladder. Bringing furniture up to the house can be difficult and would necessitate it being lightweight. In pod structures built off-site much of the furniture is built-in, and in more traditional houses the furnishing is usually minimal with a futon or mat for a bed and foldaway canvas chairs or cushions as seats.

To bring supplies and baggage up to a treehouse it is useful to rig up a basket and rope-pulley system so that goods can be placed in the basket at ground level and hauled up to the house once you have climbed safely, unencumbered and using both your hands, back up to the eyrie.

A variation on the treehouse is the stilt or pile house, which is raised above the ground or water on wooden poles or pillars that are driven into the silt of a river bed or the earth. This type of structure is found along rivers and bays and is often home to families of fishermen, but the style has been adapted to make holiday homes and hideaways on beautiful coastal locations.

Opposite, clockwise from top left *A traditional shingle technique has been used for the wall facings of this structure, which is built on a platform supported by an umbrella-spoke base. This contemporary pod house is on a freestanding base, which is accessed by a ladder via a platform. Largely camouflaged by the garden's leafy branches and shrubs, this basic plank-built house is accessed by steps or a climbing rope. A mock-tudor house has been built on a base secured among the branches of an ancient tree, but is given additional support by a series of ground-based poles.*

Building in trees

The main factor in choosing which form of treehouse construction you will adopt is the type and shape of tree in which you intend to build. Some houses are constructed on a platform that is erected independently but abuts the trunk and may use it as a support or be supported on poles embedded in the ground below. Other structures are actually built in and around the trunk and branches and will use them as an integral part of the building as if they were beams or pillars.

The freestanding but abutting style of construction is useful for treehouses built in young or slim trees such as pine and spruce. These trees may be unstable and bend or sway in a high winds and, if young, may not have branches or a trunk sufficiently developed to support the weight of a building. Large mature trees such as oaks and cedars have wide trunks and thick branches over which the weight of the house can be distributed.

When planning the construction of your treehouse also consider the weight and transportation of the building materials, and look at lightweight options such as tongue and groove or overlapping boards and corrugated galvanized steel, all of which can be attached to a wooden frame.

Above left   This treehouse is built on a platform partly set into the forks between the trunk and branches and then secured to surrounding trees. The structure is fairly lightweight so should not impair or damage the tree.   **Above**   *This more permanent style of cabin treehouse would be too heavy for the surrounding slim trees to bear, so independent buttress and bracing have been used for support*   **Opposite**   *A radial, umbrella-spoke support forms the foundation of this children's treehouse, and the building has been constructed around the trunk, so that it actually runs through the roof of the structure.*

Access

A simple, straightforward wooden ladder can be used to access a treehouse but you could create a more interesting staircase weaving through the branches and make the journey upwards part of the pleasure of getting to the treehouse. If the branches are dense and intertwined there might not be a direct route through them so access might be in stages, with a ladder to the lower levels and a series of platforms and staircases through the upper limbs of the tree. You could also have more than one way of access: for example, stairs or steps for the ascent but a rope or slide for the descent (but make sure that the area at the bottom of the rope offers a soft landing). Retractable access allows you to draw up the ladder or rope so once you are safely installed in your treehouse you can be sure of privacy and isolation.

Side rails, ropes or banister-like posts on one or both sides of steps and ladders will make access safer and give protection if ascending or descending at dusk or night-time. Wood is the material of choice for constructing access platforms and stairs because it is in keeping with the tree, but in wet weather wood can become slippery so make steps with a ribbed or textured surface or edge them with non-slip strips. Moss and lichen may also grow in cooler times of the year and you will need to scrub them off to prevent surfaces becoming unsafe.

Above left *The entrance of this low-level raised house is via a bridge-like platform to the upper storey; simple pole handrails offer some security for those using the bridge.* **Left** *This unusual sphere is suspended in the canopy of this Canadian wood and is accessed via a spiral staircase and rope bridge.* **Above** *A ladder-like stairway with railings leads from the ground to this hide-style hut. Lightweight ladders like this may be raised up and stored so that once the inhabitant is in situ the hut will not accessible by others.* **Right** *A permanent and sturdily built zigzag staircase makes for an easier, less steep climb than a straightforward ladder. It also adds to the majestic appearance of the building among the branches.*

Treehouse interiors

The inside of a treehouse should reflect its structure and surroundings, so natural materials will be a priority. Wood panels, planks, tatami or rush matting, hessian and coir would all make useful wall and floor coverings, and can be old or new depending on the style and character of your building.

Recycled mismatched panelling and planks or even scaffolding boards create a hillbilly style, and by adding different styles and shapes of second-hand windows and frames you can also enhance the informal appearance. The actual branches and trunk of the tree may also be useful and incorporated into the structure of a table or shelves, but hang and lash things to the tree rather than drilling or nailing into its wood, which may cause rot and damage over time.

If the house is primarily for use in warm weather then insulation won't be required, but if it is a year-round retreat glass windows, a floor covering and insulation for the walls will be needed. The house is exposed not only on four sides and the

Above left This streamlined contemporary interior focuses on the simplicity of life in a modern treetop home and the benefit of good storage. Here two substantial pull-out drawers in the bed base provide a place in which to keep bed linen and clothing. Left The wood-lined interior gives this building warmth and insulation and is in keeping with its location. The custom-made, built-in furniture makes use of every available centimetre of space. Opposite White-painted walls and a mix-and-match arrangement of furniture and fabrics help to give this children's playhouse a bright and lively appearance.

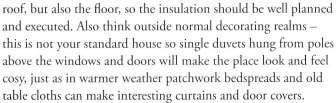

roof, but also the floor, so the insulation should be well planned and executed. Also think outside normal decorating realms – this is not your standard house so single duvets hung from poles above the windows and doors will make the place look and feel cosy, just as in warmer weather patchwork bedspreads and old table cloths can make interesting curtains and door covers.

Treehouses are usually just a small, single-room space so the interior furnishings need to be simple, stackable and lightweight. You can nominally subdivide the space into sitting and eating areas, but sitting will probably double up as a sleeping area and the eating will invariably be devoted to food preparation and washing as well. If you have electricity and water on tap then your treehouse will have an air of sophistication, but for many tree dwellers lighting will be by torch, lantern or candle, and with naked flames you must be careful in this woody, flammable environment. Water will most likely be brought up in containers, and to facilitate this a pulley system with a rope will make life considerably easier.

The motto for furnishing and decorating this type of simple dwelling is 'never try too hard'. A couple of comfortable chairs and a splash of colour is all it needs to make the place a happy and fun place to spend time.

Above left *An area of 'dead' space in the corner of the room has been used to create a cornershelf support for a basin. Varnishing the surface of the wood shelf protects it from being marked by water splashed from the basin and tap.* **Left** *The fine rattan blind behind this simple kitchen can be rolled down at dusk to prevent flying insects and small birds from being attracted by artificial lights. Oil lamps or electric light put on at dusk will attract moths, flying ants and other airborne creatures.* **Opposite** *The rail and ladder to this raised bed have been crafted from windfall wood and broken branches collected from the forest floor and woodland paths. The seasoned wood has been stripped of bark and sanded to remove splinters and roughness, but the twisted and knotted appearance of the wood has been retained to add character to the piece of furniture.*

Alain Laurens always had a fascination with treehouses, inspired by his favourite childhood book *The Baron in the Trees* by Italo Calvino. This is a tale of a 12-year-old baron called Como who, following an argument with his parents, climbs into a tree and refuses to come down. He learns to survive in his treetop realm as well as to understand the importance of freedom and intelligence.

As an adult Laurens' creative mind took him in a different direction, first as creative director of Lintas, one of Europe's biggest advertising agencies, and in time its vice-president. This high-level corporate position meant that he spent a lot of time on planes and in meetings, often working through the night, leaving him little time for his young family, let alone building a treehouse.

But after 30 years in the business Laurens decided to leave his job and settle with his family in rural Provence in the South of France, where he started the process of de-toxing from city life by planting 1,000 olive trees. While preparing the ground for planting Laurens was able to get to know his land better, and found that on a particular hill he had a spectacular old pine tree.

Provençal Treehouse

This treehouse was the result of a long-cherished dream nursed since childhood, and the inspiration for hundreds more similar constructions.

Opposite and left By building this house among the stout lower branches of the tree, just above the point where they spread out from the trunk, the weight is evenly distributed rather than focused on one point.

Above Folding, lightweight furniture and a basket-pulley for supplies add to the ease of living.

During a visit from Daniel Dufour, an old friend and colleague from his days in advertising, they started talking about Laurens's dream of building a treehouse. Dufour started to draw and after his return home he continued to draw, until some dozen or so pictures had passed between the pair.

But the dream ran into trouble when various local craftsmen and builders condemned the scheme as madness, or suggested building techniques that involved driving steel supports into the tree Laurens had selected. The project was almost abandoned until they met Ghislain André, a young craftsman who had spent 12 years training as a master of his profession. André instantly understood the need to respect and preserve the old tree and devised a belt of steel, with protective rubber lining that allowed the tree to continue growing and protected the bark.

Once the belt was safely attached 10 metres (30 feet) up the tree it then provided the foundation for Laurens's cedar-built cabin and stairway. Inside the house, furniture was custom-built to suit the single-room space, and square windows were faced with shutters so when not in use the cabin can be sealed and almost lost among the branches.

The project proved to be inspirational and Laurens, Dufour and André founded a company, La Cabane Perchée, which in 12 years has built more than 300 treehouses in Europe, Russia and the USA – for other grown-ups seeking a childlike escape ◁

Above left Window shutters provide shade, security and privacy, but because there is no glass in the frame the air and sounds of the treetops are always present and there is no sense of separation.

Above The cedar wood used in the construction of this treehouse emits oils that act as a natural preservative and that also has a distinct aroma. It is pleasant to humans but acts as a deterrent to insects such as moths, a useful device when you are up in the trees.

Opposite Built-in, dual-purpose furniture, such as a bench that becomes a bed, allows the maximum use of limited space.

Florentine Treetop Retreat

Inspired by the shape of a water tower this modern metal treehouse is built on a platform set among a small grove of trees.

Many years ago when his children were young Florence-based architect Riccardo Barthel planned to build a treehouse for them in part of his family's 2-hectare (5-acre) estate, on an olive tree-covered hill top near Galluzzo, overlooking the ancient Italian city, but the project was only realized in 2008.

'My dad built the treehouse for the family. Originally it was supposed to be for us when we were children but now we are grown-up so it has become a guest room,' explains his daughter Elena. 'We all have our own apartments or houses on the estate – my mum, grandmother, brother and his wife and I and my husband, and most are arranged around a large courtyard with a dining porch and a pizza oven. My dad and I share the same passion for "unusual buildings" and although he has designed houses in rural locations since the 1970s this was his first experiment on a treehouse. Its construction was inspired by utilitarian water towers so we call it "The Birch Tower".'

Constructed like a large greenhouse, the Birch Tower is built on a freestanding steel-frame structure of posts and a platform, like a palafitte or stilt house, and is in the centre of a group of trees rather than in one specific tree. The actual house is formed

Above Made of fine-grade steel, the treehouse has an elegant elongated vertical form.

Right The elevated position also gives access to a breathtaking view of the Florentine countryside.

Oppsite The shaded space below the house creates a generous and comfortable dining area.

Top A small, space-saving basin from a boat supplier has been fitted in to the en suite bathroom.

Above An old, cast-iron log-burning stove provides plenty of heat for the house, even in the coldest weather.

Above and opposite A blackboard headboard was fitted so that visitors could write or draw, if they felt inspired, or leave messages for each other. Three old wooden crates with castors screwed to the base provide ample storage so that the place is clutter free and the panoramic views unhindered.

of Corten fine-grade steel, insulated panels and double-glazed windows. A large French door connects the interior space with the outdoor terrace, which nestles among the treetop canopy. A wooden walkway surrounds the house and all the wood used, both inside and out, is recycled wide scaffolding boards, which have a warm colour and smooth texture, enhanced by a natural wax finish.

Inside the 16-square-meter (172-square-foot) house, which has its own electrical supply, there is a small bathroom with a large shower and a ship's hand basin. There is also a small kitchen with worktops made from marble offcuts and green drinking glasses from recycled local wine bottles. The zinc surfaces of these two rooms are also reflective, to complement the shiny steel of the exterior and maintain the modern vibe.

A few pieces of vintage furniture have been added for contrast, with the storage under the bed made from old wooden boxes. A large blackboard at the head of the bed encourages guests to leave drawings and messages, and a decorative vintage cast-iron wood-burning stove adds to the romantic atmosphere during the winter visits ◁

PART 2 **HOMES**

TO GO

on wheels

Opposite *Magical things happen when aluminium is moulded and shaped into curved sections and then riveted together – the streamlined, classic all-American trailer is built on a permanently attached chassis with highway-grade wheels and tyres.* **Above** *This vintage caravan is towed behind a similarly classic car; some people use their holiday homes to steep themselves in an era whose style they enjoy.*

Previous pages *In this portable canvas bell tent, pitched at a beach camp in Oman, the sandy floor has been stamped down and covered with locally woven mats, a thick mattress and decorative cushions.*

Defined by the *Oxford English Dictionary* as 'a house of wheels', a caravan is a portable home, one that you can take with you wherever you go. Originally pulled along by a horse, then by a motor vehicle and more recently as an integral part of a camper van or recreational vehicle, the caravan has an ancient and interesting history.

Many trace the origins of caravans to the Romani or Gypsy people and showmen. Developed in the early nineteenth century, the Romani vardo was a wooden structure that offered the travellers more protection from the elements and wild animals than the tents in which they used to live. In time the caravans became more elaborate and ornate and could take up to a year or more to build and decorate by hand.

Early caravans were utilitarian working vehicles, homes for nomads and travelling people whose work took them around the country to horse fairs or from winter pasture to summer grazing. Smaller versions were constructed as temporary accommodation for shepherds and herders who needed to watch over their flocks during lambing or periods of extreme weather.

The covered wagon or prairie schooner was the home on wheels of thousands of pioneers and immigrants who travelled across America and South Africa in search of new homes and religious freedom. Typically, a farm wagon was converted by securing six wooden arches across the base of the flat bed of the vehicle with canvas stretched securely over the frame. The suspension of the wagons was poor so many people chose to walk or ride rather than travel in the wagon, which would be drawn by horses, oxen or mules. One wagon generally accommodated a family of five, and wealthier settlers may have had additional wagons to transport their furniture, supplies and necessities for starting a new life.

Groups of settlers would often travel together for safety when heading into remote parts of the country. Some of the journeys undertaken were epic – the 1843 Great Migration saw between 700 and 1,000 emigrants travel around 2,000 miles from the east coast of America to the western states of Oregon and California.

Now a caravan is more usually a holiday home, a vehicle that leaves you free to travel wherever and whenever you want without having to rely on hotel or motel accommodation. Modern motor or mobile homes are also fitted with modern conveniences such as electric lights, refrigerators, showers, running water and even pull-out tents that can be used to create extra rooms.

In Charles Dickens' *The Old Curiosity Shop* (1840–41) Mrs Jarley is the proprietor of a travelling waxworks show. This is the description of her well-appointed van:

'One half of it . . . was carpeted, and so partitioned off at the further end as to accommodate a sleeping-place, constructed after the fashion of a berth on board ship, which was shaded, like the windows, with fair white curtains . . . The other half served for a kitchen, and was fitted up with a stove whose small chimney passed through the roof. It also held a closet or larder, several chests, a great pitcher of water, and a few cooking-utensils and articles of crockery. These latter necessaries hung upon the walls'

Opposite, clockwise from top left *This aluminium, Airstream-style mobile home is now permanently parked. The Volkswagen Camper Van, seen here with a side awning, was once the vehicle of choice for surfers who travelled from bay to bay looking for good waves. An intricately decorated Romani-style caravan with barrel-shaped roof. A traditional shepherd's hut parked in the shade of a tree.*

Streamlined living

There is something cosy and contained about a small space, but you have to be disciplined to make it work. Keep extras to a minimum and be disciplined when it comes to replacing and removing things. If you get two new coffee mugs then throw two old ones out; if you find a pile of magazines or newspapers is building up then recycle or use them to start a campfire. When you have finished using something, put it back where it came from, rather than leaving it taking up valuable space. Streamlined living makes a small area more efficient and enjoyable – if clutter starts to build up, access and manoeuvrability will be compromised, which in turn will make it a frustrating and annoying place to be.

In small spaces size really does matter. Look for small-scale and slimline furniture, don't try to squeeze a large armchair in or have a scattering of low coffee tables that you are likely to trip over. A tailor-made corner cupboard will allow you to maximize the use of every inch of a neglected area – whereas a standard-sized unit might well be a bit small or a bit too big. A box seat with a hinged top will give you a comfortable seat to sit on as well as good storage beneath.

Small spaces don't have to be dull. Colour and pattern can be part of the scheme, but don't let them overwhelm. If you are a cushion lover a few scatter cushions can be useful but when they start to reduce the sitting area of a sofa bed or chair then you have too many. But by putting two or three throws or blankets on top of each other you build in extra practicality without interfering with the purpose of the furniture.

MAKING LIMITED SPACE WORK

FOLDAWAY Look for tables with fold-down flaps, chairs that close up when not in use and even beds that clip up against a wall.

UNDER AND OVER Overhead shelves and underseat storage are often underutilized – could these strategies work for your bolthole?

STACK Pots, pans, china and glasses can all be slotted one inside another. If you're short on shelves, then don't spread things out.

HANG Rails and hooks are a great way of using wall space, from shaker peg rails to old-fashioned cup hooks or suction stick-on types.

Above, from left *Although compact most caravans can accommodate a double bed. In many vintage mobile homes the built-in wooden panelled furniture is similar to the fittings and fixtures found on boats. Splashbacks are often hinged so that they close over sinks and kitchen appliances are firmly secured so that everything is stable during transit.*
Opposite *Foldaway furniture such as these leather chairs can be stowed away when not needed to create visual space within.*

When decorating it can be helpful to pick a theme or an era on which to focus – for example, in a vintage 1940s caravan you might opt for a colour scheme that was popular at that time, such as green and cream or red and white. Look out for vintage curtains or tablecloths that will also help to evoke that time. The curtains may need to be cut down to size to fit the smaller windows of a caravan or mobile home, but the surplus could be used to make cushion covers.

If your 'home from home' is often parked or pitched by the sea a nautical or water theme might help to concentrate your attention and in a small space you can afford to go for a few good, quality things rather than a lot of space-filling cheaper goods. Bulkhead lights can be secured to a wall or ceiling and provide a good, steady source of illumination. Maps may be framed and hung on the wall or, if laminated, could be used as a table cover or as panel fronts for cupboard doors.

The use of wood, as a floor covering and for built-in units, not only is practical and durable but also serves as a background for both nautical and country-style decorative themes. For a nautical look the wood can be varnished to a high-gloss finish, or for a country feel left more mellow and aged.

Above *By keeping to a single, uniform colour or wall finish a small space will have a sleek uninterrupted feel that can make it appear larger.* **Opposite, top left** *Blinds take up less space than curtains because they can be gathered up to the top of the window, neatly out the way when not in use.* **Opposite, top right** *Table tops are often multifunctional – they can fold down flat against the wall or be lowered to create a bridge between two facing seats, creating a base for a double bed.* **Opposite, below** *This retro, mid-twentieth-century caravan features louvre blinds and roll-front units – the flexible front panels pull up and roll back behind the storage space. Both features are typical of the period.*

Traditional Shepherd's Hut

For a petite retreat that offers shelter and relaxation in one cosy space, what could be more charming than a reconditioned shepherd's hut?

This shepherd's hut may be parked in the back garden of a terraced house in south London, England, but once you are safely ensconced inside, you could be hundreds of miles away on some desolate moor or heathland (and not under the direct flight path of London's Heathrow airport).

The pale-blue painted, restored and renovated shepherd's hut is one of a number of original vehicles dating from the nineteenth century that can still be found. They were originally made as mobile shelters for shepherds who, while 'watching their flocks by night' spent long spells away from home. Built with a solid wooden frame on cast-iron wheels, the huts often have small wood-burning stoves that would have kept the shepherd and perhaps vulnerable newborn lambs, warm on colder nights, and an adjustable platform that transforms from a seat by day into a bed by night, topped off with duvets and warm blankets.

Above This efficient cast-iron wood-burning stove is fuelled by dried wood collected on long walks and stored in an old wooden crate.

Right Although parked at the bottom of an urban garden, once you are inside this hut it feels as though you are many miles away.

Opposite Foldaway furniture, such as the table and metal-framed chair, can be packed away when not in use. In former days they would have been safely secured for travelling.

Opposite and above right By day, the platform is festooned with all sizes of plump and comfy cushions, with the main part of the bed's mattress at your back. You can use themed but different patterns to create the feel you're after – a soft floral look, as here, is suited to the rustic nature of the hut. At night the base pulls forward and the back cushion slides down to create a comfortable and sizeable bed. To the right-hand side you can see the table, folded flat against the wall, and a tin bath is stored in the space beneath the seat.

Above In traditional huts the door opened in two halves so that it could be left part open to watch the flock or herd while still providing some shelter and warmth for the inhabitant. The well-stocked wood-burner makes for a toasty space, but if it gets too hot the lower part of the stable door can also be opened to let in the cooling air. Overhead shelving offers a chance to display treasured items.

Although the rustic idyll was something that Peta Waddington was keen to have as a reminder of the time she spent living in the countryside outside London, the hut now has an infinite number of guises. Sometimes her son Roy uses it to plays cowboys and indians with his cousins, with the hut becoming a pioneer's wagon heading across the prairie; at other times, it's a dance den where 'Hip Auntie', Peta's alter ego, hangs out with her collection of vinyl records. Even though her family home is just the other side of the garden, Peta felt the need for a place to escape to: 'Just somewhere different, not bound up with home life or work', she says. And that need was answered when she spotted the restored vintage shepherd's hut. When it arrived the hut was towed into place halfway down the long garden. 'We had it delivered through what was then the open end of the garden', explains Peta. 'It is now sealed off by a new brick wall', so it looks as though this little hut on wheels is here to stay ◁

Colourful Caravan

A Dutch artist allowed her creative side a free rein when it came to her second home, making all the soft furnishings and accessories by hand, and using the exterior as a canvas.

Dutch visual artist and illustrator Hanneke de Jager explains how she acquired her mobile home. 'A friend of ours had two caravans and wanted to get rid of one; he asked us if we were interested and we said yes. It was always our dream to have a caravan but hadn't envisaged one like this.'

The caravan is a 35-years-old Esterel, a French brand with hinged walls, which makes the top section collapsible. 'It always surprises people when we arrive at a campsite. We park and unfold the walls, in three minutes the roof is raised and everything inside is set up and ready to go.

'The caravan is not big, it's about 10 square metres (108 square feet), yet during our holidays we live in it quite comfortably and there is room for all three of us: me, my husband Henk and our son Matthijs as well as our dog,' says de Jager.

When the family got the caravan it was in good condition but everything was dark brown, stale and very dated. 'We replaced the floor with parquet and painted the walls white and the kitchen units bright red. I upholstered the banquette seats with plain red and a red and white gingham fabric and made curtains in a dark blue gingham so that the interior has the red,

Above **The caravan has hinged walls which fold down for travelling.**

Right **The exterior is decorated with patterns made from adhesive tape and waterproof marker pen.**

Opposite **The kitchen units were revitalized with a fresh coat of red and white paint.**

white and blue colour scheme of the Dutch flag. I made nearly everything myself – it's all been drawn, cut, pasted and sewn by hand. I even sewed the red-and-white check pendant lamp using an old vintage table doily that my mother gave me, and the rest of the tableware and furnishings comes from home,' she says.

Having sorted out the interior, Hanneke set to work on the exterior. 'I used black adhesive plastic and a waterproof marker to make the floral motifs and shapes to brighten up the panelling. It happened spontaneously, without a single working drawing in advance. For me, the caravan is like a large painting and somewhat surprisingly all the decoration has survived despite heavy rain and long trips.' And the caravan does travel – the family tow it behind their car to many destinations. 'The caravan radiates merriment and we feel on holiday from the moment we set off. It's such a cosy and deliciously relaxing place to be and it has been tailored to suit us,' says de Jager ◁

Above left In a small space every inch counts, so even the inside of the cupboards have been decorated with panels of paper and fabric.

Above The colour scheme of red, white and blue was inspired by the Dutch flag and has been picked up in the gingham fabrics as well as the choice of paint colours.

Opposite Continuing the theme, a panel of traditional Delft tiles has been included in the kitchen section. The circular lampshade was made from remnants of gingham sewn to a vintage doily.

Victorian Reading Wagon

A traditional travelling circus home has been given a smart and stylish makeover to create a well-appointed and luxurious bolthole.

They say 'a change is as good as a rest' and Felicity Loudon believes a spell away, no matter how brief, is invigorating. So when her husband is out of town on business or she just fancies a brief adventure, Felicity heads to her showman's caravan in the grounds of the family farm on the outskirts of Oxford. 'It's only a short walk from the house but it feels far removed,' she says.

The caravan is a contemporary version of a Victorian 'Reading wagon', named after the city where they were first manufactured. The compact 4.5 metre (15 feet) long and 2-metre (7-feet) wide cabin is raised high from the ground on a double-axle, steel trailer base. The exterior is clad in black-painted wood panelling and topped with a corrugated tin roof.

'Because it is mobile it can be moved to different locations during the year. In the spring it's nice to be in the orchard and in the summer by the lake, but during the autumn it needs to be close to the house so that the light and heating can be plugged into the mains electricity,' explains Felicity.

Inside, the caravan is comfortably appointed. The walls of the sleeping area are tented in black and white ticking and around the raised box bed the small windows are framed with blinds and curtains in the same distinctive fabric, so that when

Far left The short ladder leading to the front door can be removed and stored under the chassis when the hut is being towed to a new situation. There are windows on three sides, but not on the long back wall because traditionally this was the side that faced outwards as the vans were circled around as camp was made.

Left An unusual diamond-shaped window is a feature of the glossy, black-painted Dutch or stable half door.

Above The walls and ceiling are lined with black and white ticking, which insulates the interior against cold and noise.

they are drawn the interior is cosily enveloping. Floor-length curtains can be closed to separate the sleeping space from the compact kitchen with its small-scale enamel stove and ceramic sink. The kitchen units and shelves are built-in, but other pieces of furniture are designed either for sailing boats or army inspired, as in the foldaway and packable furniture used in field tents during military campaigns. Candlelight adds to the feeling of being in another place and even another time, and in the evening if it is balmy or a visitor comes for supper Felicity dines outside.

Marie Antoinette may have had her 'home from home' at Le Petit Trianon, but Felicity Loudon has hers in a Victorian wagon, and is thankfully in no danger of losing her head over it ◁

The Beer Moth

A re-purposed fire truck kitted out with an eclectic mix of furniture is a surprising and characterful home on wheels.

Through his mother's inheritance Walter Micklethwait came to run his grandparents' Inshriach estate in the wilds of the Cairngorms in Scotland, and it also became the playground for his Beer Moth home on wheels. Although brought up as a city boy in the east of London, Micklethwait spent many holidays at Inshriach House, exploring in the surrounding wild countryside.

'Before I came to work on the estate I was in the antiques business for a number of years, but always had a passion for old vehicles,' he says. After a long search and a couple of near misses Micklethwait tracked down a 1956 Commer Q4, which he bought from the Manston Fire Museum in Kent and kept in store until he moved to Scotland to look after Inshriach

'It's a rugged outdoors vehicle so perfect for the rugged outdoors, and because it is pre-1960 doesn't require an MOT, is tax exempt and is insured as an historic vehicle so makes it very cheap to run. Also it has a maximum speed of 45 mph so you can't go anywhere quickly, which is ideal for this terrain.'

Micklethwait's first idea was to make the truck into a bar rather than a holiday home. 'The roll-up canvas sides means that you could easily serve drinks from it and I called it the Beer Moth

partly because it was a play on Bar Fly, and sounded as though it could have some vague Norse mythological connection. But I looked the words up in a dictionary of urban slang and it means "someone who steals drinks in a bar", which suited as the truck is a bit of a petrol guzzler.'

But instead of a bar Micklethwait turned it into a movable retreat. He laid down a floor of oak parquet rescued from a Tudor mansion; salvaged snooker table slate creates a hearth beneath the Rayburn stove and he installed a Victorian double bed frame with a new and very comfortable orthopaedic mattress.

'I also had the canvas panels made to my design by a manufacturer who makes covers for historic vessels, relates Micklethwait. 'They had made panels for other vehicles but this was a high spec with flaps to cover the windows and leather straps to tie up the sides. In the winter I'm taking the Beer Moth back to the workshop to add straps to the furniture and to adjust the bed so that it is more roadworthy for longer journeys. As it is you have to park on a bit of a slope to make the bed level and because of the spring suspension it can be a bit bouncy when you walk around inside' ◁

Opposite **The rugged Commer Q4 with one of the custom-made canvas panels rolled up to reveal the well-equipped interior.**

Top **The living accommodation includes a cast-iron stove, a Chesterfield chair and a Victorian bedstead.**

Above **A painted sign denotes the truck's original use.**

Railway Carriage at Rest

For a train buff what could make a more perfect retreat than a piece of railway history, painstakingly and knowledgeably restored with a eye both for comfort and sensitivity to its original use.

Antiques expert, author and broadcaster Paul Atterbury came across a 1903 railway carriage by chance when he was looking for somewhere to live in Dorset. 'What we found was the carriage with a couple of old beach huts being used as individual rooms all set in a big, overgrown garden,' he says.

'I had a childhood passion for trains and had seen houses made from railway carriages, so owning one was a chance not to be missed and when this one came along I was actually writing books about railways and railway history. What appealed to me most was that the carriage was original and unaltered.'

Built in 1903, the six-wheeler Great Western Railway (GWR) company carriage is about 10.5 metres (35 feet) long and 2.75 metres (9 feet) wide and made from mahogany panelling on an oak frame, all mounted on an iron chassis. Where the panelling had rotted Atterbury replaced it with marine ply. The scheme he used for the paintwork was an adaption of original GWR colours.

'When we bought the carriage there was a rather unreliable source of electricity, a single cold tap and the lavatory was an earth closet at the end of garden. The floor was the original wood and in good condition so we simply sanded it clean.

Above The renovation of the railway carriage inspired the collection of railway-related ephemera such as enamel freight tags.

Right The exterior has been lovingly restored.

Opposite A dining room now occupies a section of carriage previously taken up by seating.

Opposite The addition of a stove surrounded by a simple mantle created a focal point for the sitting room.

Above The original door from the corridor now opens into a bedroom.

Above right Although the internal partition separating the corridor from the compartments has been removed, the outside doors are still intact.

I put in a wood-burning stove, hot water, a kitchen and a kind of bathroom, added a porch at the back and then converted a garden shed into a bedroom for our two young children. We lived in it, mostly at weekends, and then over the years added to it bit by bit, including a proper bathroom.

'Once the carriage was habitable we started collecting railway memorabilia; it seemed appropriate as decoration. It was fun finding the signs, which came largely from second-hand shops and auctions, and we were always on the lookout for smaller pieces of furniture because the carriage doorways are narrow and difficult to manoeuvre things through.'

The carriage and adjacent rooms were used by the family all year round. 'Whenever we did repairs we added insulation to the walls and the wood-burning stove made it very snug in the winter. The carriage is a wonderful, magical and romantic place. We always loved being there' ◁

Contemporary Shepherd's Hut

A traditional design is given a modern makeover that encompasses all of the compact neatness of the original design with sleek and skilful detailing.

James Noble built his own shepherd's hut because he was too tall to stand upright in the traditional design. 'The shepherd's hut is a little piece of history and I didn't want to mess with that, so I based my hut on the original but made it bigger, but not so big that it couldn't be towed behind a car,' he explains.

Noble's hut is 2.4 metres (8 feet) wide by 3.6 metres (12 feet) long, mounted on the base of an old horse box and made from larch and oak with roof tiles of recycled aluminium drinks cans. He created the rib-like pitched ceiling by soaking wooden batons in water and, once they were pliable, bending and clamping them into shape, leaving them to dry in situ. Between the batons the roof is clad with canvas and insulated with sheep's wool, while the lower walls are finished with tongue and groove panelling. All the furniture is built-in; a comfortable sofa converts into a double bed, a hinged table clips neatly against the wall when not in use and there is a two-shelf kitchen with a gas hob. The gas canister for the hob is stored outside under one of a pair of bench seats; under the other is a finely executed lavatory seat ◁

Above James Noble created a leaf-like wooden top to fit over the trailer bar transforming it into an outdoor dining table, covered by a colourful canvas awning.

Right In a second hut Noble built for his children to sleep in, a smaller indoor table, locked up against the right-hand side of the canvas-clad wall, folds down when needed, while the seat converts into a bed.

Right The canvas-clad walls are insulated with Herdwick sheep's wool. There is a small but efficient log-burning stove which works so well, in conjunction with the wool insulation, that the hut can be used all year round.

Far right Two gas rings and a bench provide simple but adequate cooking facilities.

Below The roof tiles are made from recycled aluminium drinks cans and the clinker-built wooden frame allows water to run freely off the exterior.

under canvas

Opposite *Guy Mallinson's hand-built his yurt has a canvas, rather than wool felt, outer covering and a raised wooden walkway to the front door.* **Above** *This tipi is in a leafy location in a wood in Dorset, England. The tipi is set on a raised deck to provide a level footing and to keep it dry and as insect free as possible.*

Tents are one of the oldest forms of shelter constructed from a wooden frame covered in durable material such as animal hide, sticks or tightly packed rushes. These portable homes were used by nomadic people and could be quickly assembled wherever they made camp.

From the nomadic peoples' tents there developed a range of canvas-covered frames. Canvas is a plain, heavy-duty fabric used for sails, canoes and backpacks, so was already widely used by explorers and the military. Canvas tents became more sophisticated and were designed with guy ropes and tent pegs to make them secure and sturdy and the material was treated to make it waterproof, flame retardant and mould resistant.

Among early canvas tents is the Sibley, patented in 1858, and named after its inventor Henry Hopkins Sibley, who based his design on the tripod construction of the Native American tipi. The northern Scandinavian Lavvu tent used by the Sami peoples is also of a similar style and structure.

Often confused with the tipi is the Native American wigwam which, like the Mongolian ger and central Asiatic yurt, is rounded. These domed one-room dwellings, known as the wigwam in the American northwest and as wickiups in the southwest, are formed from arched wooden poles covered with grass, brush, mats, hides or cloth, and many are beautifully decorated with tribal motifs and symbols.

Most modern tents are made from synthetic materials such as polyester and polyethylene, with taped seams, aluminium poles and nylon ropes. They also come with a choice of frames made from rigid or flexible poles or with in-built pop-up struts. Modern materials and frames mean that tents are lightweight, so are easy to carry, assemble and pack down.

You can also build up a tent to suit your needs; for example, there is the single skin with one waterproof layer of fabric forming the roof and walls. This is ideal for warm, dry areas and will accumulate little or no condensation on the inside. If you are likely to camp in a rainy or damp area then add a flysheet that can be suspended over the single skin tent for added protection. For cool and damp areas a double-skin tent may be the best option. This is a waterproof outer tent which may have a built-in groundsheet, and which fits over a second internal tent. The two layers of tent with a slight gap between them will also provide extra insulation and warmth.

Opposite, clockwise from top left *At night the internal light silhouettes the lattice and spoke-frame structure of this contemporary, canvas-covered yurt. Canvas can be used in conjunction with more permanent building materials, as shown here with a corrugated roof. The mesh inner layer, or fly screen, over the entrance to this tent allows air to circulate and light to penetrate but keeps insects and animals out. This colourful modern tent is raised off the ground on a platform with legs, making it warmer and less prone to damp inside.*

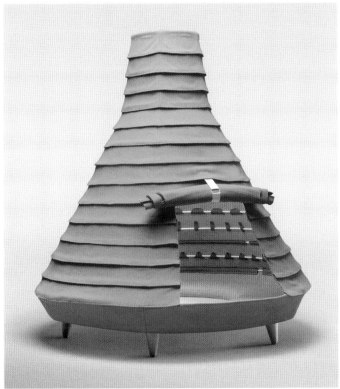

Sleeping under the stars

Above *The traditional felt-covered yurt is a substantial structure, which in its native regions is used for periods of up to six months before being dismantled and transported to the next area of grazing. This canvas version is lightweight, easy to move and to re-erect, but is spacious inside and tall enough to stand up in.* **Above right** *This unusual ridge tent has the wooden frame on the outside and the canvas hung within it; it is more usual for the canvas to be put over the frame.* **Opposite, top right and far right** *Simple awnings can provide protection from the sun.* **Opposite, below** *A classic ridge tent is elevated above ground level on a wooden platform so that it will be cooled by good air circulation and less likely to be visited by insects.*

When you make a home under canvas you can absorb your surroundings, lose yourself in the landscape. Tents are light-weight and portable so you can go way off the beaten track, away from car horns and mobile phone signals and from light and air pollution, giving your mind and soul a real rest. Part of this total relaxation is to allow all your senses to come in contact with your surroundings. Canvas, whether in a simple tent or a more insulated yurt, provides only a thin barrier between you and the great outdoors. It will give a little shelter from the elements and protection from the wildlife, but it is minimal.

Lying in your tent you will hear the wind in the trees, bird call at dawn and dusk, the scurrying of small creatures through the scrub and undergrowth. At night certain flowers and trees become intensely aromatic. Wild herbs also release their scents when you brush against them with your clothes or trample them underfoot. If you know your flora and fauna, or have a reliable guide, then pick the herbs and wild fruits and taste them; bring some back to your campfire and use them to flavour your food.

Sitting outside your tent at various times of the day you will be able to watch the landscape to see how it changes, how shadows fall or clouds move across the sky and how it changes from the rose-tinted gold of sunrise to midnight blue and starry silver at night. You will also be able to touch the rough bark of the trees, the velvety moss on cool damp stones or the warm sand beneath your feet, really getting a sense of where you are.

Living under canvas

There are three types of camping. The first is the semi-permanent option, like the nomadic tribes people who move seasonally from one area of pasture to another and pitch a tent or yurt for several months. This type of canvas living will start with levelling off and stamping down the earth, then laying down a waterproof membrane and a thick layer of hay or rush or a wooden floor. This will give the structure a firm, damp-proof base and good insulation. The floor may then be covered with rugs, mats or hides to give softness and warmth.

Because of the length of time spent in this type of canvas dwelling it is worth furnishing it with more permanent fittings. For example, a timber bed frame, which can be dismantled for transportation, and a futon-style mattress, which can be rolled up and carried, will provide a comfortable night's sleep. Fold-up canvas or leather chairs and chests and boxes, in which goods can be stored and carried, will double as tables and stools.

The second type is transient camping, where people are hiking or moving each day from one place to another. Here the rules are that you don't take anything that's surplus to requirements, and everything you take must be portable. So for this type of camping you need a groundsheet, an inflatable mattress or foam mat, a sleeping bag, stove and maybe a fold-up chair, plus a knife, fork and spoon, mug and plate and saucepan – anything else you can make or find, or just do without.

Opposite *Beneath an attractive frame of bent wooden poles supported on a lattice base, this modern interpretation of a yurt has a simple but well-furnished interior.* **Left** *For more permanent canvas dwellings it is worth laying down a good floor over a resilient membrane or tarpaulin – this will provide protection against insects and make a firm base on which to arrange furniture and equipment.* **Below** *Although a single, open space, the area within this ridge tent is adequate enough to accommodate a full-sized bed, a defined sitting and dining area as well as a stove with a hearth.*

The third type of camping is holiday style and this can be fun rather than purely practical. The serious trekkers and outdoorsmen may keep to camouflage and earthy-coloured tents and equipment, but for those who are spending just a few nights under canvas you can make your 'home from home' as colourful and decorative as you like. If you are camping at the bottom of the garden or near enough to a parking area that you can easily unload a car, then make comfort a priority. Fold-up beds will have more 'give' than a sleeping bag on the ground and a duvet will wrap around you but allow more manoeuvrable space than the confines of a tubular bag.

Cushions may seem a bit of an unnecessary luxury but they are versatile and can double as pillows and back rests as well as making sitting on the ground more comfortable. In fact, a couple of good plump cushions and the back support of a tree can make fold-up chair unnecessary.

Another accessory that makes a night under canvas more comfortable is a mosquito net. Not only does it look romantic but if carefully arranged around the bed before dusk it will also keep insects away from the bedding. When ready for bed, dim any lights before opening the net to get into bed, so that flying insects aren't attracted to the light's glow.

If camping on a commercial site or at a concert or event it might be worth taking something that makes your tent easily identifiable among the others – for example, a flag or homemade bunting that you can attach to the frame. It will add to the fun appearance of your tent and also make it easier for you to give friends a description so that they can find you. Saying 'meet us at the green tent' when there are 30 other green ones in the field is not helpful, but if you say 'The green one with the bunting made out of old curtains' then you are much more likely to be spotted.

Above left *You can use tents as individual rooms; here one is used as a bedroom while another, like the one opposite, could be used for food preparation and dining.* **Left** *Foldaway camp beds are more comfortable than a basic sleeping bag on a mat on the ground. Kitted out with a duvet and pillow and arranged beneath a mosquito net a good night's sleep is almost guaranteed.* **Opposite** *Storage can be attractive too; if you're not carrying things for long distances. then wicker and straw baskets will do the job and can be hung up from the frame of the tent using butchers hooks or bungee cords, which will keep their contents dry and safe from bugs and beetles.*

Craftsman Camping

When furniture designer and maker Guy Mallinson relocated from London to Dorset he brought with him not only his cabinet-making skills but also knowledge gained while working on new wood-bending technology.

Above Sited next to a fishing pond 'Hoppus', a tipi, has its own shower and toilet in a separate cabin, and sits in the centre of a deck with planks that radiate out from the base like the spokes of a wheel.

Above right Raised wooden walkways ensure boots and shoes are relatively clean and dry when they reach the tent.

Opposite In the bell tent 'Fipple', the flue of the wood-burning stove is ducted through the side of the tent; the area of canvas directly in contact with the flue has been bound with a protective insulation tape.

As Mallinson's knowledge and interest in the local woodland grew he set up a series of woodworking courses among the trees. To provide a place for students to take a break he constructed a shelter made from old parachutes suspended from stout branches and erected a bell tent as a canteen. The tent proved so successful that he bought another and pitched it at the bottom of the woods by an ancient boundary of old trees.

Mallinson christened the 5-metre (16-feet) bell tent 'Fipple', after the plug that constricts the airflow in end-blown flutes, and set about making it a comfortable and enjoyable place to stay. First a firm and solid deck was laid to provide warmth and insulation, then a secluded sitting out area was created under an old willow and a meandering path laid to Fipple's doorway, all of which contributes to the feeling that the bell tent is more than just a temporary put-you-up. The path and base all around the site of the tent has been laid with a thick layer of sweet-smelling wood chippings to keep the access clear and the tent interior as clean and mud free as possible.

The interior is also furnished, with a wood-burning stove, coir matting and a proper king-sized bed. There is an outdoor shower and access to electricity, which makes it viable to stay in the woods from spring to early autumn. 'But the tent is still portable. We pack it up and take it away during the summer and it comfortably accommodates the whole family,' Mallinson says.

Mallinson's interest in tent-making also produced a traditional tipi. He chose this type of tent because of its central height, which makes it less back breaking for adults to stand up in. Named 'Hoppus', after the traditional measurement used for timber before the introduction of metric units, this 7-metre (24-feet) circumference wood-frame tent is also large enough to accommodate a king-sized bed and a log-burning stove, taking it into a category above your usual canvas tent.

'The poles are 10.5 metres (35 feet) long and made from softwood "thinnings" harvested from local woodland,' explains Mallinson. 'We then stripped the bark from the wood with a drawknife and left the clean poles to dry and season for a winter.'

The ground in the area is soft so Mallinson devised a double-layer platform on which to erect the tipi and secure the poles. 'The top deck is larch wood, which is naturally rot resistant and the supports on which it stands are blocks of sweet chestnut. The two layers of deck also prevent rainwater from seeping in to the tent, because it runs off the top layer and doesn't lie or puddle.' Between the upper and lower decks Mallinson inserted a layer of fine mesh to keep insects from getting into the tipi and he also adapted the traditional, central open-hole ventilation system to avoid rainwater coming through.

'Originally we constructed the tent with the traditional round "door" opening cut into a mid-section of the canvas wall with an exterior, protective roll-down panel, but I tripped over the raised base section so often, and found the panel regularly left unsecured, so I redesigned the entrance with a proper door. Although it looks a bit Flintstone-like, it works well,' explains Mallinson The outer skin of the tipi is made from military-grade waterproofed canvas, secured and kept taut by ashwood pins ◁

on water

Opposite *On sheltered inland lochs and lakes where the water is contained and less prone to the turbulence of violent storms a simple contemporary structure like this provides a comfortable, yet mobile living space.* **Above** *This homemade floating house anchored off shore makes little concession to conventional boat design, and could equally be erected on dry land.*

Recreation and relaxation on the water is a popular pastime, but for the more adventurous who want to get away from a land-locked existence there are more interesting ways of doing so than booking a berth on a hotel-style cruise liner or joining a flotilla of boats travelling en masse. To get a different perspective of life on the water take a look at recycled commercial vessels that in the past have ploughed their wares through thousands of nautical miles of waterways and along rugged coastlines.

In Britain there is a distinctive vessel called a narrowboat, designed specifically for use on the narrow British canal system; these boats were built to be no more than 2.13 metres (7 feet) wide. Although restricted in width the families who made these boats their homes, as well as their source of livelihood, developed a style of naive painting that they used to embellish the few possessions they could keep on board. The paint initially provided weatherproofing for wood and metal objects but then became a decorative feature.

Traditional narrowboat painting was applied to the panels of the cabin and three main utensils: the Buckby can (a drinking water container), a bowl with handle for scooping water from the canal and the nosh bowl from which the horse that pulled the boat ate his oats. The paintings often featured castles set against snow-capped mountains, said to resemble the Carpathian Mountains of Eastern Europe. Colourful roses were a popular motif as was the stylized eye symbol often seen on fishing boats in Greece and Portugal.

The barge, like the narrowboat, is also a working vessel but mainly for river and continental canal transport. These vessels were built with a broader, flat-bottomed hull to give it more stability when laden with cargo and to allow them to sail through shallower waters. In the early Industrial Revolution, canal and river transport held its own against the newly arrived train. In fact, the canal system and boat haulage are credited by economic historians with boosting the commercial worth of New York to such a position that it overtook Philadelphia as America's largest port and city. But the cost of dredging and maintaining the canal system and the increasing speed of the trains meant that waterways declined as a major source of commercial transport.

Barge and canal systems were nonetheless of great, perhaps even primary, economic importance until the 1920s, especially in Europe, the Low Countries, France, Germany and Poland. In France, the canals have now become an important source of tourist revenue – for example, the Burgundy Canal, which connects the Atlantic Ocean to the Mediterranean Sea, is a major international vacation destination.

Light vessels and lightships have also been surpassed by modern technology and satellite systems, with the United States Coastguard saying farewell to their last lightship, *Nantucket 1*, at the end of March 1985. Although large and difficult to sail without an experienced crew, these sturdy vessels can be moored, and the cabins and decks, where the crew once lived and worked, can be transformed into unusual and interesting holiday homes.

Opposite, clockwise from top left *This is a hybrid, part caravan and part boat. It can be towed behind a car and then launched into a lake; it also has a retractable roof and is fitted out with a table, two bench seats and a fridge. Old working vessels, such as a lightship, a postal service boat or a paddle steamer can be converted into interesting mobile homes. Many narrowboats and barges were used as cargo vessels as well as homes for their owners, now the cargo areas are no longer needed, the living accommodation can expand into the hold. Some floating homes are more house than vessel and designed to be moored on calm lakes rather than destined for high sea adventures.*

On board

A wide variety of vessels can be used as 'homes from home'. There are the purpose-built cabin cruisers and yachts, some vintage with many nautical miles under their hulls, and others newly built with all the very latest in gadgets and technology. There are boats more suited to the protected waters of lakes and inland waterways while others, such as trawlers, are purpose built to withstand salty spray and turbulent seas, so when setting out to buy or rent a boat choose the type that will suit your lifestyle and purpose.

If your idea of fun is to bob along on calm waters and dangle a fishing rod over the bow, followed by a restful night's sleep moored by a grassy bank, then you are probably looking for a vessel appropriate to lake or waterway sailing. If on the other hand you are focused on adventure and distant travel, then you need something more robust, as well as the navigational skills with which to steer and map read.

Modern ships come with streamlined cabins and advanced systems for solar power and water desalination; while older vessels may lack these advancements they will have buckets of character and history. As well as the cost of buying the vessel you will also have to factor in the maintenance. For new vessels this should be relatively modest as the materials used in construction will usually be synthetic resins and fibreglass, which are robust and saline resistant. Old timber or metal hulls will need to be dry-berthed for regular scraping and repainting. If you plan to own a vessel outright you will also have to factor in mooring costs, which in a busy marina can be expensive.

But for all the practicalities and expenses, life on board can be liberating and enjoyable. The environment and nature will play a part in daily life. If you are on a narrowboat and passing through the canals that link one industrial town to the other, then the landscape will be urban, whereas travelling through the rural canals in the south of France will give a mellower outlook.

The weather will also be a major factor in daily life on board. If you are at sea you need to constantly monitor the situation, so that if a storm is in the offing you can make for the shelter of a harbour or cove. If on a narrowboat going through a series of locks taking you from one level to another, it is a far nicer task on a warm, sunny day than on a cold and icy one, but you should always be ready for every type of climate. Have on board everything from high-factor sun protection to warm fleeces and windproof jackets, as well as full wet weather gear and waterproof boots (good storage on a boat is essential).

Above *Although life on board can be cramped you can always get off and stretch your legs. With shallow draught boats you can anchor so close to shore that you can swim or wade to the beach. With boats that need to be moored further away a kayak or rowing boat will be required to transport belongings and supplies.* **Opposite** *Originally used as cargo vessels for transporting goods, as well as a home for the crew, narrowboats are now mainly used as a 'home from home'. Although only basic navigational skills are required to steer them along canals, you will need to know how to operate locks.*

Left *This American MetroSHIP houseboat consists of a rectangular box on a shallow hull; this type of top-heavy construction is not viable for sea voyages but is suitable for mooring in a sheltered cove or bay on a lake or river. The living quarters are constructed from Japanese-style opaque panelling and wood-framed clear glass doors; the simplicity is Zen-like and relaxing.* **Below** *The furnishing and fittings of the living quarters are minimal, streamlined and inspired by New York loft living, with a central island unit that incorporates the kitchen sink and storage and a dining area that doubles as a desk. The finish and detailing of the interior are to a very high standard and the vessel is powered by two outboard motors.*

Below deck

The style of interior decoration you choose for your boat will depend on your personal taste, but may also be influenced by the type and age of the ship and where it will be moored. The ferry opposite is based in New York City harbour, a bustling metropolitan area, and its interiors reflect this, being filled with colourful baskets, rugs and furniture, whereas the MetroSHIP, which looks out on a more tranquil, leafy riverbank, has a calmer, sleeker selection of fitted and freestanding furniture.

The interiors also reflect the ages of the vessels; the ferry is over a hundred years old and converted from a working to a domestic environment, while the MetroSHIP is new and purpose-built for contemporary living. It is fitted with HD TV, internet, a Danish sound system, Gaggenau and Viking kitchen appliances, a full-size shower and laundry facilities, as standard.

Both boats could easily be changed: a scattering of coloured cushions, a rug and some glassware on the MetroSHIP would give it more personality, while the editing of domestic trappings on the ferry could take it back to its workman-like roots.

Above *This 1907-built one-time Ellis Island ferry, briefly fitted with guns and used by the army in Boston harbour during the First World War, is now a family home and studio space for decorative artists. Currently moored in New York City harbour, the boat was restored and given a new lease of life by its owners Richard and Victoria Mackenzie.* **Right** *Due to the scale of the ferry, the 'rooms' are a good size and can accommodate accessories and embellishments. In the cabin the varnished timber ceiling and door panels allude to the ferry's age and previous use. The bed and desk are recent introductions and would not be practical in a moving vessel.*

Luxury South Seas Cruiser

Eric Booth describes *Maha Bhetra* as 'a villa on water' and it is where he and his family and friends come to escape the heat and bustle of their homes and offices in central Bangkok.

Eric is the director of Thai Silk Company, owner of the Jim Thompson brand, a job that has seen him revamp its design portfolio global profile. But life on board the *Maha Bhetra*, which is moored in the Andaman Sea in the southern reaches of the Bay of Bengal, is the ultimate relaxation.

'We spend time fishing, birdwatching and diving or just watching the turtles, marlin, sailfish and at night, luminous plankton. You can wake up in a different bay or cove each day without having to pack a bag or queue for airport security,' he says.

The name *Maha Bhetra* is Pali Sanskrit for Big Boat, and this vessel, which looks like a cross between a Chinese junk and the *Black Pearl* of *Pirates of the Caribbean* fame, was designed by New York-based architect Ed Tuttle, who co-owns it with Eric's mother Patsri Bunnag. 'The boat is mainly constructed from teak, it is heavy and stable, built for comfort not speed,' says Eric.

With a crew of five and four double berths for up to eight passengers the boat can travel at nine and a half knots and stay at sea for up to eight days at a time, making trips to Hong Kong and Singapore accessible. There are several decks and levels with sitting out areas, some covered with awnings, others open.

Above **Maha Bhetra** sailing on the Andaman Sea.

Right The lounging area on the upper deck is open-sided.

Far right Louvred windows in one of the cabins on the lower deck filter sunlight and allow sea breezes through.

Above right The well-appointed bathroom in a guest cabin.

'Everyone can find their own space,' says Eric, 'you can read quietly or be in a more sociable group. When you spend days together it is important to have time and room to be apart.'

Because the climate is balmy the boat has been constructed with sliding walls of louvre panels that give privacy and shade but allow cooling breezes to pass through. The boat was also designed to have spacious rooms rather than cabins, although in true nautical style most of the furniture, such as the platform beds and bench seats, are built-in so that they are secure while at sea.

While the external appearance of the boat is solid and masculine the internal dressings are luxurious and elegant. 'The aim was to blend contemporary style with Asian culture, using colours such as black, brown and taupe with spicy highlights of cinnamon and orange,' says Eric.

On the deck at the prow of the ship, towelling-covered padded mats are laid out for those who wish to sunbathe and lounge, and there is an outdoor shower to wash off salt after diving or swimming off the deck. 'After a week or even a long weekend on the *Maha Bhetra* your body and senses are completely refreshed,' says Eric ◁

Classic 1930s Sailing Boat

A beautifully fitted vessel with compact, streamlined furnishings is a retro retreat for a woman with a passion for sailing.

Above *Blade* in all her glory, sailing on the river Debden, a tidal estuary in Suffolk.

Right The main saloon cabin has walls panelled with gleaming polished wood and elegant cream soft furnishings. The brassware light fittings are typical of boats of this vintage.

Bryony Hebson and her late husband Robert shared a passion for boats. 'We lived on a houseboat when we were first married, then we owned a lifeboat and a sailing boat. We weren't great sailors – it was more for the fun of owning one and being on the water,' she says. On her husband's death Hebson sold their last boat but after several 'landlocked' years found that she missed the freedom of having a 'home from home' on the water, so having set up a bed and breakfast business at The Old Granary Cottage in the East Anglian riverside town of Woodbridge, she looked for another vessel.

After much searching, Hebson came across *Blade*, built in 1939 by Smith Bros of Goole for Sydney Kirkham, then managing director of the Hippodrome Theatre in Sheffield – the name *Blade* is said to have been his tribute to the steel manufactured in the town. Carvel-built with pitch pine planking and a mahogany

transom, she is a classic and very elegant motor launch, with all the fittings you would expect of a vessel of that era.

Since she was built the boat has had only four owners. One, Dick Smart, kept detailed notebooks of the works and maintenance he undertook and when Hebson bought the boat the notebooks came too. 'They are invaluable as well as funny,' she says, but admits that having a son, Laurence, a qualified shipwright, makes the costly upkeep of the boat possible.

With the boat safely moored in Woodbridge on the Debden River and the exterior of the boat under her son's supervision, Hebson turned her attention to the interior, upholstering the seats and bunk mattresses in plain cream linen and adding a few nautical-themed, patterned cushions. 'Everything has its place and there is no room for clutter,' she says, so there are just a few well-chosen antiques among the many original fittings.

Above left The view through the length of the boat below deck shows the 'heads', or lavatory, on the left.

Above The galley kitchen shelves have either a raised rim or a bar to hold glasses and china secure during choppy weather. The stainless steel sink and drainer are practical and easy to maintain.

Above right, clockwise from top left Brass and copper echo the burnished gleam of the golden wood that predominates on board. The ship's bell in the wheelhouse bears the boat's name. Carefully selected antique and nautical-themed accessories have been used to dress the boat. A compact corner sink in the heads makes optimal use of a tight spot.

There are also practical, modern additions, including a couple of small electric heaters, which make it comfortable to stay on the boat in the winter, as well as custom-made canvas winter covers for wind protection. 'When I can, I take *Blade* out on a trip, but I need a crew of friends or family and generally Laurence is the skipper. We cruise the Debden and enjoy the scenery, but my ambition is to cruise the French canals,' says Hebson ◁

Psychedelic Barge

From the traditional black and white exterior you would never guess that the *Leviathan*, a working Birmingham Canal Navigation butty built in 1899, has such a bright and contemporary interior.

The 21-metre (70-feet) boat, moored on the Kennet and Avon Canal, is entered from the stern, and is arranged so that you pass from one space to the next. The bespoke, hand-crafted living space with curving intertwined panels of pale, polished ash and oak gives the narrowboat an almost organic appearance. From the stern you go through the white bathroom with a sunken bath, and on into the engine room. After that there is the main living area where a full-height, industrial metal-clad door leads through to a reception space and kitchen.

Beyond the kitchen is a sitting area with a curvaceous sofa on spring-like, coil legs and finally through to an office. There is additional seating immediately in front of the bed, which is raised up on a platform in the bow, and under the bed is hanging space and a series of drawers.

Now with luxurious groovy-feeling accommodation for two, the *Leviathan* has come a long way from its days as a sooty coal-powered workhorse, and latterly as a passenger boat; it has become something of a decadent haven that moves along the inland waterways at a leisurely pace ◁

Above The plain exterior of the *Leviathan* retains its appearance as a working craft.

Right Short sections of partition help to break up the longitudinal, corridor-like form of the interior.

Opposite The organic and surprisingly bright decoration of the cabin includes swirling wood panels and lots of red.

Refitted Lightship

A former workhorse of the sea has been lovingly restored and adapted to become a stylish great escape with an industrial vibe.

B uilt in 1938, Lightship 93 spent her working life at sea, first as a manned vessel, then automated and finally, before being decommissioned in 2004, partially solar powered. The various stages saw alterations to her structure. First the crew's cabins and mess area were closed off and the wheelhouse removed, then the front and aft holds were pumped full of expandable filler and finally solar panels were placed on the foredeck.

And when she had served her time and was no longer wanted by Trinity House, the official General Lighthouse Authority for England, Wales and British territorial waters, she was 'pensioned off' at auction. Italian-born photographer Michele Turriani bought the hulk and had it towed back to east London, where he started on transforming the working vessel.

Turriani camped on board to get an idea of how he might make the space work. 'I've had my bed in every part of the ship,' he says, and admits that there was no grand design. The work happened by default and as time would allow. But with patient and careful research and a great deal of dogged determination

Opposite Vintage leather armchairs and furniture with a patina of age were chosen to complement the working history of the ship.

Above left The bright red painted lightship as she is today., in her latest incarnation.

Above Portholes and raised doorways are part of the ship's ocean-going heritage.

he has now restored and adapted most of the ship. 'My main rule was that whatever I brought on board had to be nautical or industrial to be in keeping with the working ethos of the vessel,' he says, so he scoured naval scrapyards in Devon, eBay, junk shops and even local skips. 'It was difficult to find an electrician willing to put in the effort to rewire and install some of the older fittings and the chunkier bulkhead lights,' says Turriani.

The galley kitchen is fitted with vintage 1950s English Rose kitchen units bought from eBay. 'They had been painted but I stripped them back to the metal,' he says. The floor is new: 'Reclaimed timber was expensive, often comes in short planks and has residual nails so I bought new wood but didn't seal it. It was left to get gloriously dirty for a year and then oiled.'

Zinc metal ducting conceals pipework and cabling that would have been difficult to attach to the metal beams and girders, and exposed copper pipes lead to the shower over the reclaimed, double-ended zinc bath, all of which adds to the working and industrial appearance below deck. Using original drawings given to him by Trinity House Turriani was able to see what alterations had happened during the ship's working life and then he added a few adaptations of his own. Portholes that had been filled in were reopened and in other areas doorways were cut through 40 millimetre (1½-inch) thick steel panels.

'A sculptor friend helped me by making shutters that close over the openings between the bathroom and sitting area and above the main stairs to the lower deck. They are metal and in some cases riveted so that they fit in with the feel of the ship,' he says. In fact, it is the only clue to some of the work that Turriani has done to the ship – original panelling is held in place by stout rivets while more recent work has been soldered so has a visible smooth seam to indicate the join.

An almost invisible trapdoor in the galley floor is lifted by a brass D ring to reveal a steep flight of stairs disappearing into the belly of the ship. Down here, behind a sealed doorway, unopened for 20 years, Turriani found the crew's quarters, with the original built-in mahogany bunks and cupboards, a few still with their brass handles. It is as though the crew had just packed their kitbags and gone ashore. Even if moored securely to a harbour wall, Lightship 93 still offers an escape for the imagination as well as from the troubles of life on dry land ◁

Above, from left to right Hatches open up to reveal stairways between the decks. The vintage 1950s English Rose kitchen units were sourced on eBay and then stripped back. In the bathroom utilitarian units combine with exposed copper piping.

Far left A recycled office chair with a broad wheeled base is now used as a dining chair.

Left The ship is permanently moored so things are less likely to roll off open shelves.

PART 3 **THE ESS**

ENTIALS

Adaptable and built-in furnishings

In cabins, boats and caravans space is limited and often the amount of kit and equipment needed to enjoy activities permitted by these sorts of dwellings is bulky and difficult to contain, so designing the layout and fitting of furniture is something of a balancing act. On one hand you want enough room to move around and function comfortably while you sleep, eat and rest, but on the other hand you need to be able to keep all the belongings you require, close to hand.

One option is built-in furniture; this allows you to work around difficult shapes and obstacles while making the most of every available inch or millimetre. The simplest example is the box window seat, which can be configured to fit into a bay window or a recess, or simply along a flat wall.

The seat can be designed with a hinged top that lifts to give access to the storage space beneath, or it can be made with two large, deep drawers on rollers that are easily pulled out from beneath the seat. A third option is simply to leave the space beneath the seat without a fitting so that the maximum amount of stuff can be stored with flexibility, but shielded from view by hanging a simple decorative curtain.

Above *Bunk beds work well in a long, narrow room; they take up a minimal amount of space while leaving a passageway free to walk through and space beyond for bookcases.* **Right** *A coffee table was made from a recycled agricultural feeding trough and a couple of old planks of wood.* **Opposite, left** *Foldaway furniture saves space and can be brought out on demand, it is also lightweight and easy to transport.* **Opposite, right** *This built-in cupboard on board a ship was originally used as a locker for a crew member's kit and possessions, although utilitarian it is made of good-quality varnished wood and polished brass handles.*

Shelves can be put up over doorways or above head height at the perimeter of a room, and bunk beds will always take up less floor space than two, or even three, single beds, because they are stacked one above the other.

Dual-purpose furniture is also useful – a stool that doubles as a table, tables and chairs that can be brought indoors but are weatherproof enough to be left outside, and a blanket box or trunk that works well as a coffee table while having the internal capacity to keep a winter duvet and extra pillows out of the way.

Furniture can also be constructed from things that have had a previous use. Old milk crates turned upside down and topped with a cushion make serviceable stools for children; old wooden boxes, packing cases and tea chests make reasonable side tables in a rough and ready fashion and even planks of salvaged wood can be used to construct a table top.

A solid plain door laid on a pair of trestle legs or matching stone pillars will produce a dining table, and wooden garden trellis can find a new role as infill for cupboard doors or as indoor screens and partitions. The best idea is to look at what is available and then think about how to use it. When decorating your retreat don't be limited by the normal necessities of furniture and design; it's your space so anything you like goes.

Freestanding furniture

Old and recycled furniture and accessories make great choices for a 'home from home', but there comes a point where you have to choose whether to keep the old, worn finish or revamp with a coat of paint or a wad of sandpaper and a pot of wax.

First evaluate the piece: is the faded finish part of the character and appeal of the item? Does it need so much repair and filler that most of the original appearance will be lost and finally where will it fit? Are you putting it in a fresh, brightly painted room where it will look out of place, or is it going among other vintage and second-hand pieces where a brightly painted, shiny piece of furniture would be incongruous?

Scale is also important, especially in caravans, huts or yurts where there is usually just one all-purpose living room. A large dining table will only work if there is enough room to walk around it comfortably and if it has a second function, so that as well as somewhere to eat it is also a part of the kitchen and used for food preparation. Similarly a large cupboard is useful storage, but an end panel can also be used to hang things from and the top will also support boxes or a wine rack.

Above from left *An old crate is used as a footstool while a basket hanging from the wall doubles as a bedside table without taking up floor space. By painting this spacious cupboard blue it blends in with the walls and appears less dominant in the room. Natural linen curtains and a throw complement the antique chair and old wood of the walls and floors. The worn paint and rust spots give these chairs a mellow and relaxed appearance.* **Far Left** *Although showering, whether outdoor or in, is more economic in terms of water and power use there is nothing quite as relaxing as a hot, scented bath, especially after a long day's hiking or a day spent collecting and chopping wood, so every once in a while it is good to indulge and a deep, old-fashioned roll-top bath is the perfect place to do it.* **Left** *Scaled-down furniture is ideal for a child's play space.*

Storage

By providing well-positioned and appropriate storage you will make it easier to keep things tidy. Try to fit storage to the location or task with which it is most frequently used. For example, to keep a limited run of kitchen worktop uncluttered try storing condiments and spices in a wall-mounted basket or rack rather than on the surface; they will still be close at hand but not in the way. Suspend a roll of kitchen paper under an overhead unit or at the end of the worktop rather than on an upright stand. Don't store kitchen utensils in a worktop jar – put up a wall rack or chain from which they can be suspended.

An ample linen press on the landing between bedrooms is useful because when you are making up the beds the clean sheets are easily accessible from the adjacent rooms. And to make the linens easy to identify label single and double sheets and hand and bath towels so that you can quickly spot what it is you are after. Also, in a house with two or more floors hot air from the lower levels will rise, so putting a linen closet upstairs helps with the airing process of the freshly pressed linens. Try placing bunches of dried lavender or rosemary between the linens and they will become scented while they are stored.

In mobile homes such as caravans, boats and barges storage needs to be secure. Cupboard doors may require additional fastenings or bolts to ensure that their contents don't push against the door and force it open, then spill onto the floor.

Above A deep drawer can be built under a small window seat and used to store books, tea towels, hats and scarves or, in a kitchen, packets of dry ingredients. **Right** *These shelf racks on board a ship have small wooden panels that pivot and slot into a niche in front of the plates and bowls, holding them securely in place.* **Opposite, clockwise from top left** *Labelling what is stored in a cupboard or on a series of shelves makes it easier to find what you are looking for. Four rows of hooks screwed to the inside of a door make a useful store for enamel mugs. By raising a bed up onto a purpose-built storage unit you can double the amount of available floor space in a room.*

For temporary restraints try elastic bungee cords. These covered stretchy ropes have a single or multi claw at each end and can be threaded through door handles or around a pile of rugs or blankets and then clipped to something stable or secure. Then, when you have arrived at your location, the claws can be released and the bungee cord removed and stored until next time it is needed.

A larger version of the box window seat is the box bed base, which not only elevates the bed above the floor but makes use of the space underneath. This often overlooked space can accommodate larger items such as suitcases, rucksacks and bulky winter bedclothes. If you store a mix of fabrics and outdoor clothing or equipment bag them up separately so that the down duvet doesn't get stained with roller skate oil or walking boot dubbin. And with all storage, make sure you regularly take everything out and clean the darkest corners of the cupboard or shelf. These warm, dark nooks are perfect nesting places for small creatures and insects when it gets cold and nasty outside.

Heating

Although it is possible to heat a hut or house with an electricity supply by simply flicking the switch of a radiator or underfloor heating unit, there is something much more atmospheric and rewarding about lighting a fire. Whether the fire burns in a stone-rimmed pit outside or indoors in a cast-iron stove or fireplace with chimney, the sounds and smell of a real fire are magical. For dwellings used in cold or wet seasons and for periods of more than a few nights, a cast-iron stove with flue is an effect and economic way of providing heating.

The flue is designed to duct smoke out of the building, but its metal casing also retains and conducts heat, so not only is the log-burning belly of the stove providing warmth, the flue does too. If this type of stove is not raised on legs it is advisable to place it on a base of fire-retardant material, especially if it is sited on a wood floor. A fireplace can also be fashioned out of clay and baked hard. The damp clay is moulded around a brick-built hearth or metal grate with a flue or chimney, then a small fire is built inside. This gradually dries the moisture from the clay, forming a firm casing in which regular fires can be built.

Below left *Clay has long been used to fashion fireplaces and ovens, but the damp clay needs to be dried slowly and cured before a full fire is set, otherwise the clay dries out too quickly and cracks.* **Below** *A metal base mat separates the bottom of the wood-burning stove from the surrounding wooden floor.* **Opposite, clockwise from top left** *The glass front panel in this stove allows the glowing flames to be seen while the embers are contained. With its long, flat top panel, this log-burning stove can also be used for slow cooking casseroles or heating breads and pies. Only use specifically sourced and supplied wood for burning; don't just chop down the nearest trees for logs. A basic camp-fire provides heat, protection and somewhere to cook.*

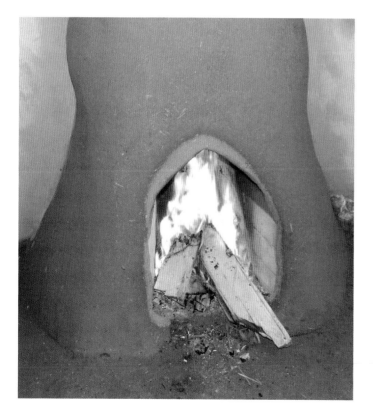

Lighting

Conventional lighting can be run on mains electricity or power from a generator, and also by power from solar panels, but if none of these is available, or you just fancy a softer more romantic light, candles and oil-powered lanterns are an option. With electrically powered lighting it is important to check regularly that the cables and plug points are safe. During times when a house or cabin is shut up mice may invite themselves in and chew through wiring. When closing up a building for any length of time turn off all power switches and disconnect plugs from sockets, and if an area is prone to damp remove light bulbs too, as the metal base can rust and stick into the fitting.

Scented candles, such as citronella, provide attractive light and help ward off biting insects. Candles should be burned in a protective container, which need be no more sophisticated than a jam jar – this will contain melting wax and prevent the flame from being blown out. Oil-burning lanterns should be filled with care, as the fluid is highly flammable. Position them carefully so that they cannot be accidentally knocked over.

Above left *A multi-functional floor-standing lamp with adjustable heads can be used to highlight the painting on the wall while also supplying light for reading in bed.* **Above** *In bathrooms a contained light fitting is safest; this type of fitting fully encloses the bulb and prevents any contact with water or moisture.* **Opposite, clockwise from top left** *Oil lanterns have an integral handle for safe carrying without burning your fingers, but the handle can also be used to fix the lantern to a hook on a ceiling beam or window frame to provide overhead or a higher level of lighting. Individual adjustable lights allow a person at one side of the bed to read, while the other sleeps, or to focus one light on the ceiling for a softer, more diffuse illumination, while the other provides lighting for the bed. In buildings created from flammable materials such as straw or wicker make sure your light is safely enclosed and contained.*

Cooking

'Homes from home' are places where you can indulge in a different type of living, where you can enjoy a lifestyle that favours a change of cooking style or meal scheduling. In this relaxed and informal setting you can gather and build up a kitchen as you go along and as you accumulate more possessions and stores that need to be accommodated over time and repeated visits to your bolthole.

When away from your routine life, meals can be more carefree and informal: a loaf of bread, a lump of cheese and a bottle of wine thrown in a rucksack is all you need for a delicious al fresco lunch – no plates required. Casseroles and slow-cooking dishes can be put in the bottom of an oven at low temperature and left all day, so that when you return from a day long trek up a mountain a delicious hot pot is ready to serve with a thick chunk of bread and a quickly tossed salad.

Outdoor cooking can be great fun too. Experiment with ideas from native peoples and other cultures: try wrapping fish or bananas in broad waxy (and non-poisonous!) plant leaves (or tinfoil), laying them in a hollow in the ground and covering with embers, or spit roast over an open fire. Barbecues can be done on equipment as simple as an oil barrel cut in half, or as sophisticated as a temperature-controlled stainless steel grill.

Opposite, clockwise from top left *A simple chimney ducts smoke and steam away from a couple of gas rings on a clay-built base. This kitchen has been created from a collection of freestanding units, racks and a wall-mounted cube of box shelves. The hot plate on top of a range can be used to boil a kettle, fry bacon and eggs and make toast.* **Left** *A gas canister with a stand can be used to heat a kettle or a billycan of soup or stew.* **Above** *A range is also useful for cooking dishes that require long periods at low temperatures such as hot pots and casseroles, which can be left to bubble away while you are out.*

Eating

Catering for life in the great outdoors can be divided into three categories: food to go; food to take; and outdoor catering. Food to go is the nourishment you take with you; it should be simple and tasty as well as suited to your activity or location. For example, if cycling, kayaking or hiking. your meal should be created to be hand-held, rather than eaten off plates with cutlery that requires carrying. Sandwiches and rolls are staples, but wraps and pies can also be good. Always take plenty of drinks, ideally water, and if out in the cold a vacuum-flask of hot soup, tea or coffee is always welcome and warming.

Food to take is a meal transported by car, caravan or boat so it can be more elaborately presented, but ideally pre-prepared and cooked, such as salads and platters of sliced fish, meat or cheeses. Outdoor catering is food that you eat when you get back to base; it can be cooked indoors or out but will be close to running water and a *batterie* of kitchen utensils.

Above left *Unbreakable tableware made from melamine or plastic is perfect for picnics and for carrying in unstable vehicles and boats. It is also lightweight and easy to pack.* **Above** *The boot of a car or the back of a camper van can provide a useful area on which to prepare a meal away from sand and insects. You can also work standing up rather than on your hands and knees or stooping over a bag or box.* **Opposite** *Being back at base doesn't mean you have to eat indoors. Make a table outside with a couple of planks of wood and some trestles and enjoy the remains of the day while sipping a glass of wine and eating good, locally sourced foods.*

Suppliers

TRY IT . . .
places to stay

Canopy & Stars
Tel +44 1275 395447
www.canopyandstars.co.uk

Cool Camping
www.coolcamping.co.uk

One off Places
www.oneoffplaces.co.uk

Wanderlusts
Tel +44 7815 439130
www.wanderlusts.co.uk

Yurts and tents

Mawgan Porth Yurts
Tel +44 1637 860322
www.mawganporthyurts.co.uk
Contemporary canvas yurts

Bridge and Wickers
Tel 020 7483 6555
www.bridgeandwickers.co.uk
Tents with private deck and hot tub at
Minaret Station in New Zealand

Feather Down
www.featherdown.com
Set in Ambrosia Farm, Bridgewater New
York State, USA with hardwood floors
and log-burning stoves

Stepped Travel
Tel +44 1258 880980
www.steppedtravel.co.uk
From the country that makes tents for
the great and the good, Rasa in Jaipur,
India has a range of canvas homes from
home, complete with air con

Frontier Canada
Tel +44 20 8776 8709
www.frontier-canada.co.uk
Near the Bedwell River in Clayoquot,
Vancouver Island, Canada. Twenty tents
with a cookhouse

The Ranch at Rock Creek
Montana, USA
A 6,000 acre ranch with riding and
biking as well as tents
Tel + 1 877 786 1545
www.theranchatrockcreek.com

Umpqua Lighthouse State park
Oregon, USA
Tel +1 800 452 5687
www.traveloregon.com
On the Pacific shoreline – there are six
well-appointed yurts

Caravans and Airstreams

Belrepayre
Ariege, France
Tel +33 5 61 68 11 99
www.belrepayre.com

Shooting Star Drive-in
2020 West Highway, Escalante
UT 84726, USA
Tel +1 435 826 4440
www.shootingstardrive-in.com

The Grand Daddy Hotel
38 Long Street, Cape Town
8001 South Africa
Tel +27 21 424 7247
www.granddaddy.co.za
Airstream rooftop caravan park

Roulotte Reatreat
Tel +44 845 0949729
www.roulottereatreat.com
French Roulotte caravans are spacious
and have beautifully carved wooden
exteriors – four can be found at Melrose
in Scotland

Pods

Cornish Secrets
Tel +44 845 0949729
www.cornishsecrets.co.uk
Geodesic domes and other luxury
glamping locations

BUY IT . . .
a place of your own

Shepherd's huts

Peachey Dovecotes
Tel +44 1373 813992
www.peacheydovecotes.com
Gerry Peachey creates huts and follies
and is available for commissions.

James Noble at Wiltshire Wagons
Tel +44 1672 851336
www.puckshipton.co.uk/wagon
Unique and individual, Noble's huts are
curvaceous and of his own design

Cowley Shepherds Huts
Tel +44 1242 870411
www.cowleyshepherdshuts.co.uk
Clad in wood or corrugated tin with
reclaimed pine floor board, shepherd's
huts are made to order by Theo in the
Cotswolds

Treehouses

La Cabane Perchée
Tel +33 490 75 9140
www.la-cabane-perchee.com
'Grownup' tree houses constructed
around the world

Squirrel Design
Tel +44 1454 238967
www.squirreldesign.co.uk

Cheeky Monkey Treehouses
Tel 01403 732 452
wwwcheekymonkeytreehouses.com

Yurts

Yurts Direct
Tel +44 20 8144 7275
www.yurtsdirect.com
Makers and supplier of traditional style
felt-lined yurts

The Really Interesting Tent
Company
Tel +44 1803 873297
thereallyinterestingtentcompany.co.uk
Devon based maker or yurts and large
tents

The Colorado Yurt Company
Tel +1 800 288 3190
www.coloradoyurt.com/yurts
Available in five sizes and with floors

The Rainier company
Tukwila, Washington, USA
Tel +1 425 251 1800
www.rainier.com/yurts
Family owned and operated yurt
building business

Sheds

www.readersheds.co.uk

www.shedworking.co.uk

Plaster, clay and rammed earth

Adobe Factory
Tel +1 505 853 4131
www.adobefactory.com
Supplier of adobe bricks and products

Clayworks
Tel +44 1326 341 339
www.clay-works.com
Specialize in contemporary clay work
and design

Cob in Cornwalll
Tel +44 1326 231773
www.cobincornwall.com
Build new cob structures and repair
traditional buildings made in the
material

Log cabins

Strongwood Log Homes
Tel +44 117 244 0080
www.strongwoodloghomesuk.com
From 690 sq ft cabin to a house with
many bedrooms, thyey can create a
home from home from the foundations
to giving you the key

Appalachian Log Homes
Tel +1 800 726 0708
www.alhloghomes.com
supply cabins in kit form that you can
erect yourself or they will do it for you

Coventry Log Homes
Tel +1 603 747 8177
www.coventryloghomes.com
From small chalet style cabins to house
size

DRESS IT

Accessories and dressings

RE
www.re-foundobjects.com
Vintage cushion covers and quilts

Toast
www.toast.co.uk
Oil lamps, throws and home wares

Baileys
Tel +44 1989 561931
www.baileyshome.com
A wide range of practical and traditional
things from brushes to buckets

Habitat
Tel +44 844 499 4686
www.habitat.co.uk
Contemporary accessories rugs and
cushions

Anthropologie
Tel +44 800 0026 8476
 www.anthropologie.co.uk and USA
www. anthropologie.com
Bohemian style colourful accessories

Oka
Tel +44 844 815 7380
www.okadirect.com
A wide range of wicker and basket
products

Mini Moderns
 www.minimoderns.com
Retro style prints and designs, some
wonderful seaside themed designs in
fabrics, paper, paints, rugs and cushions

Skandium
Tel +44 20 7584 2066
www.skandium.com
For more pared back and Nordic designs

Zara Home
Tel +44 800 260091
www.zarahome.com
Bed linen, bath towels and table ware

Felt
Tel +44 20 8772 0358
 www.feltrugs.co.uk
Ideal for Yurts and long term tens homes
wool felt floor cushions, rugs and scatter
cushions from Kyrgyzstan in bright
colours and geometric patterns

The Biggest Blanket Company
Tel +44 20 7823 4338
 www.biggestblanket.co.uk
From tartan rugs to cashmere throws

Ian Mankin
Tel +44 0 7722 0997
www.ianmankin.co.uk
An endless supply of sturdy cotton
ticking, natural stripes and indigo denim
fabrics

DECORATE IT

Paints and finishes

Farrow & Ball
Tel +44 1202 876141
www.farrow-ball.com
Many mellow and unusual shades

Little Greene
Tel +44 845 880 5885
www littlegreene.com
Highly pigmented paints with a great
depth of colour

EarthTech
Tel +1 303 465 1537
 www.earthtechinc.com
Environmentally friendly paints

Old Fashioned Milk Paint Co.
Tel + 1 978 448 6336
 www.milkpaint.com
Paint formulated to the recipes used by
Shakers and Colonial homemakers

Auro Organic Paint Supplies
Tel +44 1799 584888
 www.auro.co.uk

Nutshell Natural Paints
Tel +44 1364 73801
www.nutshellpaints.com

Davis Colours
Tel +1 323 269 7311
www.daviscolours.com
Pigments for colouring concrete floors

Floors and old wood finishes

Crucial Trading
Tel +44 1562 743 747
 www.crucial-trading.com
Natural fibre floor coverings made from
sisal, jute and coir

Generations
Tel +44 1509 210 321
wwwgenerationsinc.co.uk
Hand-planed oak flooring

The West Sussex Antique Timber
Company
Tel +44 140 3700139
www.wsatimber.co.uk
Planks, panels and parquet and offer a
full joinery service

Drummonds
Tel +44 1428 601103
www.drummondsflooring.co.uk
Architectural recycling specialists have a
constantly changing stock of flooring

Center Mills Antique Floors
Tel +1 717 334 0249
 www.centremillsantiquefloors.com/
Salvaged and recycled panelling and
flooring

Natural Cork
Tel +1 706 733 6120
www.naturalcork.com
Natural cork has a warmth and
insulating quality for both walls
and floors

Wincanders Cork Flooring
Tel +1 201 265 1407
 www.wicanders.com

DLW Linoleum
Tel +1 717 397 0611
www.armstrong.com
Linoleum is an old-fashioned product
that has seen a fashionable revival and
is ideal for areas where muddy boots or
wet feet and frequent.

Forbo Industries
Tel + 1 800 842 7839
 www.forbo-industries.com

Forbo-Nairn
Tel +44 1592 643777
 www.forbo.co.uk

Recycled, vintage and salvaged materials

Retrouvius
Tel +44 (0) 208960 6060
 Tel www.retrouvius.com
From wooden crates to banister spindles
and from light fittings to coat hooks, the
supply is constantly changing

LASSco
Tel +44 207749 9944
 www.lassco.co.uk
At a series of locations this reclamation
company has something from
everywhere

American Salvage
Tel +1 305 836 444
www.americansalvage.com

COMPANIES AND INDIVIDUALS FEATURED IN THE BOOK

24 H Architects
Hoflaan 132
3062 JM
Rotterdam
Tel +31 104111000
www.24h.eu

Axel Vervoordt Company
Kanaal, Stokerijstraat 15 –19
2110 Wijnegem
Belgium
Tel +32 3 355 33 00
www.axel-vervoordt.com

Riccardo Barthel
www.riccardobarthel.it
(web site under construction)
info@riccardobarthel.it

Baumraum
Andreas Wenning (Architect)
Borchersweg 14
28203 Bremen
Germany
Tel + 49 4 21. 70 51 22
Mobile +49 176. 700 24 383
www.baumraum.de
a.wenning@baumraum.de

Big Sur Getaway
Clear Ridge Road / Hwy 1
Big Sur, CA 93920
USA
www.bigsurgetaway.com
reserve@bigsurgetaway.com

Bubble Tree
6 rue Lionel Terray,
92500 Rueil-Malmaison
France
Tel +33 9 77379150
www.bubbletree.fr

La Cabane Perchée
Alain Laurens
Tel +33 4 90759140
www.la-cabane-perchee.com

Canopy and Stars
The Old Farmyard
Yanley Lane
Long Ashton
Bristol BS41 9LR
UK
Tel +44 1275 395 447
www.canopyandstars.co.uk
bookings@canopyandstars.co.uk

Casey Brown Architecture
Level 1 l 63 William Street l
East Sydney NSW 2010
Australia
Tel +61 2 9360 7977
www.caseybrown.com.au

CCCA Architects
Ken Crosson
L1, 15 Bath Street
PO Box 37-521
Parnell, Auckland
New Zealand
Tel +64 9 302 0222
architects@ccca.co.nz

Cob Courses
Edwards & Eve Cob Building
White Cottage, The Common
Fleggburgh
Norfolk NR29 3DF
UK
Tel +44 1493 369952
Mobile/Cell 07949 241815
www.cobcourses.com
sheepie32@hotmail.com
charlotteevemusic@hotmail.co.uk

Lesley Craze Gallery
33– 35a Clerkenwell Green
London EC1R 0DU
Tel 044 20 7608 0393
www.lesleycrazegallery.co.uk
info@lesleycrazegallery.co.uk

Cwmhir Court
www.cwmhircourt.co.uk
Featured in The Silo on pages 72–75.

Dunton Hot Springs
52068 Road 38
Dolores
Colorado 81323
USA
Tel +1 970 882 4800
www.duntonhotsprings.com
info@duntonhotsprings.com

Robin Falck
Helsinki
Finland
Tel +358 40 482 9299
www.robinfalck.com
mail@robinfalck.com
Designer of the micro cabin featured on
page 7 and page 188 right

Linda Felcey
www.lindafelcey.com
Artist. Featured on page 10.

Claire Fletcher
www.clairefletcherart.com
Illustrator and artist. Featured in
Vintage Beach Hut pages 44–47.

Free Spirit Spheres
420 Horne Lake Road
Qualicum Beach BC
Canada V9K 1Z7
Tel +1 250 757 9445
Mobile/Cell 250 951 9420
www.freespiritspheres.com
rosey@freespiritspheres.com

Ian Garlant
Tongavegen 24
Hatlestrand 5635
Kvinnherad
Norway
Tel +47 9769 1802
http://ianwardgarlant.com

Hausman Hughes
office@hausmanhughes.co.uk
Featured in The Tin House pages 64–67.

Hawthbush Farm
Gun Hill
East Sussex TN21 0JY
Tel: + 44 844 9911601
www.hawthbushfarm.co.uk
enquiries@hawthbushfarm.co.uk

Hidden Hideaways
Mount Pleasant Cottage
Mount Pleasant Street
Penzance
Cornwall TR19 6SA
Mobile/cell 07887 522788
www.hiddenhideaways.co.uk
info@hiddenhideaways.co.uk

Hive Modular
211 St. Anthony Pkwy – Suite 104
Minneapolis
Minnesota 55418
USA
Tel +1 612 379 4382
www.hivemodular.com
info@hivemodular.com

Hanneke de Jager
Kastanjesingel 28
3053HM Rotterdam
The Netherlands
www.hannekedejager.com
Illustrator. Featured in Colouful
Caravan pages 140–143.

Jim Thompson
www.jimthompson.com

Lakes Cottages
Tel +44 176 875 8652 / +44 153 989
7455
www.lakescottageholiday.co.uk
info@lakescottageholiday.co.uk

Felicity Loudon
Tel +44 1367870400 for appointment
www.theprivatehouse.com
Soft furnishings and accessories.
Featured in the Reading 'Retreat' pages
144–45.

Made in Hastings
madeinhastings.co.uk

Mallinson Ltd
Higher Holditch Farm
Holditch
West Dorset TA20 4NL
UK
Tel +44 1460 221 102
www.mallinson.co.uk
contact@mallinson.co.uk

Mermeladae Studio
Gloria7 3º,3ª,
08902, L´H,
Barcelona
Spain
Tel (+34) 934328202
www.mermeladaestudio.es
info@mermeladastudio.es
Featured on page 157 below left.

MetroPREFAB
David Ballinger
Tel +1 818-357-4000
www.metro-ship.com
david@metroshed.com

Michael Micklethwaite
Inshriach House
By Aviemore, Inverness-shire
Tel +44 1540 651341
www.inshriachhouse.com
Featured in The Beer Moth pages
146–47.

MT under Canvas
21004 St Joe Rd
Havre
MT 59501
USA
Tel +1406 219 0441
www.mtundercanvas.com
info@mtundercanvas.com

Old Granary Cottage B&B
Tel +44 1394 383793
Featured in Classic 1930s Sailing Boat
pages 176–79.

Paperback Camp
Irena & Jeremy Hutchings
571 Woollamia Road
Woollamia NSW 2540
Australia
Tel +61 2 4441 6066
www.paperbarkcamp.com.au
info@paperbarkcamp.com.au

Peter Quinnell
www.peterquinnell.com
Featured in Vintage Beach Hut pages
44–47.

Silvo Rech and Lesley Carstens
32B Pallinghurst Road, Westcliff 2193
Johannesburg
South Africa
adventarch@mweb.co.za

Sealander GmbH
Holtenauer Straße 96
24105 Kiel
Germany
Tel +49 431 160 700 81
Mobile/cell 176 313 88 127
www.sealander.de
info@sealander.de

Catriona Stewart
www.catrionastewart.co.uk
Artist and designer. Featured in Snug in
a Bothy pages 96–99.

Tongabezi Lodge
Private Bag 31
Livingstone
Zambia
Tel +260 213 327450
www.tongabezi.com
reservations@tongabezi.com

Treehotel/ Brittas Pensionat
Edeforsvag 2A
960 24 Harads
Sweden
Tel + 46 928-104 103
www.treehotel.se
info@treehotel.se

Michele Turriani
www.shootspaces.com
Featured in Refitted Lightship pages
182–85.

Vintage Vacations
Tel +44 7802 758113
www.vintagevacations.co.uk
anything@vintagevacations.co.uk

Peta Waddington
www.petawaddington.com
Graphic designer and DJ. Featured
in Traditional Shepherd's Hut pages
136–39.

weeHouses
Alchemy
856 Raymond Avenue, Suite G
St Paul
MN 55114
USA
Tel +1 651 647 -6650
www.weeHouses.com

**Wiltshire Wagons and Wiltshire
Wagon Holidays**
Puckshipton House
Beechingstoke
Pewsey
Wiltshire SN9 6HG
Tel +44 1672 851336
www.puckshipton.co.uk/wagon.html
noble.jj@gmail.com

The Yurt Retreat
Fordscroft Farm
Fordscroft
Crewkerne
Somerset TA18 7TU
UK
Mobile/Cell: 07773 505 671
www.theyurtretreat.co.uk
relax@theyurtretreat.co.uk

Index

Figures in italics indicate captions.

Credits

1 Taverneagency.com/ Photographer: Anouk de Kleermaeker/ Producer: Hanneke de Jager; 2 Jacqui Small LLP; 3 Taverneagency.com/ Photographer: Susanna Blavarg / Producer: Paul Lowe; 4 Getty; 6 The Interior Archive/ Simon Upton; 7: Robin Falck, Helsinki, industrial based designer; 8 - 9 Guy Mallinson/ www.mallinson.co.uk; 10 Artist retreat and studio designed by Markus Blee for Linda Felcey www.lindafelcey.com; 11 above Getty; 11 below www.vintagevacations.co.uk; 12 above Luis Garcia; 12 below Getty; 14 left Getty; 14 right Designer: Pierre Stephane Dumas/www.BubbleTree.fr; 15 The Interior Archive/ Tim Beddow; 16 left Taverneagency.com/ Photographer: Colin Cooke/ Producer: Paul Lowe; 17 Getty; 18 Sindabezi Island, Livingstone, Zambia www.tongabezi.com; 19 Tongabezi Lodge,Livingstone, Zambia www.tongabezi.com; 20 Getty; 22 Ben Rahn/ www.aframestudio.com; 24 Mickey Muennig Alan Weintraub/ arcaidimages.com; 25 James Balston/ office@hausmanhughes.co.uk; 27 above left The Interior Archive/ Simon Upton; 27 above right Christophe Madamour/ Hemis.fr; 27 below left Getty; 27 below right James Balston/ office@hausmanhughes.co.uk; 28 Greg Vaughn/ Alamy; 29 above left Jacqui Small LLP; 29 above right The Interior Archive/ Nicolas Tosi; 29 below Jacqui Small LLP; 30 Interior Archive/ Simon Upton; 31 Jacqui Small LLP 32 left Nigel Hicks/ Alamy; 32 right The Interior Archive/ Simon Upton; 33 above left Ray Main/ Mainstreamimages/ Las Banderas; 33 above right Getty; 33 below GAP Interiors/ Mark Scott; 34 hivemodular.com; 35 Logan Macdougall Pope/ VIEW; 36 left The Interior Archive/ Simon Upton; 36 right Lakes Cottage Holidays; 37 above right The Interior Archive/ Nicolas Tosi; 37 below Taverneagency.com/ Photographer: Jim Hensley/ Producer: Nina Dreyer; 38 Ben Rahn/ ww.aframestudio.com; 39 Jacqui Small LLP; 40 left Jacqui Small LLP; 40 right The Interior Archive/ Simon Upton; 41 left Jake Fitzjones Photography/ Claire Peters; 41 right The Interior Archive/ Simon Upton; 42 above left Narratives/ Photo: Alun Callender / Owner: Stene & Ulrika Magnusson; 42 below left Jacqui Small LLP; 42 below right Narratives/ Photo: A. Mezza & E.Escalante; 43 above The Interior Archive/ Simon Upton; 43 below Alchemy LLC; 44 - 45 Jake Fitzjones Photography/ Claire Peters; 46-47 left Taverneagency.com/ Photographer: Nathalie Krag/ Producer: Tami Christiansen; 48 - 51 Taverneagency.com/ Photographer: Dana van Leeuwen/ Producer: Jessica Bouvy; 52 – 55 The Interior Archive/ Michele Biancucci; 56 - 57 www.duntonhotsprings.com; 58 - 59 Paul Raeside/ Ian Garlant; 60 – 63 Darren Chung/ Lesley Craze/ jewellery designer and gallery owner www.lesleycrazegallery.co.uk; 64 – 67 James Balston/ office@hausmanhughes.co.uk; 68-71 Taverneagency.com/ Photographer: Mikkel Vang/ Producer: Jessica Bouvy; 72 - 75 James Balston/ www.cwmhircourt.co.uk; 76 Narratives/ Photo: Brent Darby; 77 Roland Halbe Fotografie; 79 above left Lakes Cottage Holidays; 79 above right GAP Interiors/ Costas Picadas; 79 below left Nicolas Matheus/ The Interior Archive; 79 below right Getty; 80 Getty; 81 above Bodrifty Roundhouse, available to hire from www.hiddenhideaways.co.uk/ Photographer: Ian Kingsnorth; 81 below Narratives/ Photo: A. Mezza & E. Escalante / Owner: Cartucho Antoraz & Susana Bárcena; 82 The Interior Archive/ Fritz von der Schulenburg; 83 left Taverneagency.com/ Photographer: Mikkel Vang; 83 right David Clapp/ arcaidimages.com; 84 Narratives / Photo: A. Mezza & E. Escalante / Owner: Raúl & Elsa Cheli; 85 www.edwardscobbuilding.com/ comwww.cobcourses.com; 86 The Interior Archive/ Mark Luscombe-Whyte; 87 GAP Interiors/ Costas Picadas; 88 left Narratives / Photo: A. Mezza & E. Escalante / Owner: Raúl & Elsa Cheli; 88 right The Interior Archive/ William Waldron; 89 above left The Interior Archive/ Alex Famsay; 89 below left www.hawthbushfarm.co.uk/ Molly Mahon; 89 below right The Interior Archive/ Nicolas Matheus; 90 The Interior Archive/ Nicolas Matheus; 91 above left GAP Interiors/ Costas Picadas; 91 above right Narratives/ Photo: A. Mezza & E. Escalante / Owner: Cartucho Antoraz & Susana Bárcena; 91 below The Interior Archive/ Nicolas Matheus; 92 – 95 Andreas von Einsiedel/ Axel Vervoordt; 96 - 97 Paul Massey/ Mainstreamimages; 98 - 101 Adam Butler/ Mainstreamimages; 102 – 105 The Interior Archive/ Andrew Wood; 106 The Interior Archive/ Tim Beddow; 107 Photo: Peter Lundstrom, WDO - www.treehotel.se; 109 above left Getty; 109 above right baumraum/ Andreas Wenning/ www.baumraum.de; 109 below left Lucinda Lambton/ arcaidimages.com; 109 below right Getty; 110 left & right Getty; 111 Getty; 112 above left Jerry Pavia/ Red Cover/ Photoshot; 112 above right Getty; 112 below FREE SPIRIT SPHERES Inc.; 113 Michael Ventura/ Alamy; 114 above Photo: Peter Lundstrom, WDO - www.treehotel.se; 114 below Jacques Delacroix/ Treehouse designed by Alain Dufour; 115 www.ipcsyndication.com; 116 above Martin Desjardins/ Oredia/ Lived In Images; 116 below Narratives / Photo: Jan Baldwin / Makalali Private Game Lodge, South Africa; 117 Francj Schmitt/ Oredia/ Lived In Images; 118, 120 left & right, 121 Andreas von Einsiedel/ Alain Laurens; 119 left & right Luc Wauman/ hemis.fr/ Lived In Images; 122-125 Taverneagency.com/ Photographer: Nathalie Krag/ Producer: Tami Christiansen; 126 Credit: Tandem Photography/The Interior Archive. interior of a bell tent at a beach camp organized by Hud Hud Travels at Al Khaluf, Oman; 128 www.vintagevacations.co.uk; 129 Douglas Keister/ Sheltered Images/ Lived In Images; 131 above left & below right Getty: 131 above right Taverneagency.com/ Photographer: Robbert Koene/ Producer: Liezel Norval-Kruger; 131 below left Simon Bevan Copyright Country Living/ Hearst Magazines UK: 132 left Evan Sklar/ Red Cover/ Photoshot; 132 right & centre, 133 www.vintagevacations.co.uk; 134 The Interior Archive/ Roger Davies/ Designer and Owner Jane Hallworth; 135 above left Adrian Briscoe Copyright Country Living/ Hearst Magazines UK; 135 above right Simon Bevan Copyright Country Living/ Hearst Magazines UK; 135 below Caroline Brandes/ Big Sur Getaway; 136 - 139 Chung/ Mainstreamimages/ hipauntie.com; 140-143 Taverneagency.com/ Photographer: Anouk de Kleermaeker/ Producer: Hanneke de Jager; 144 – 145 Paul Raeside/ Felicity Loudon; 146 – 147 To book a stay at The Beer Moth go to www.canopyandstars.co.uk (Photographer: Sophie Burry); 148 - 151 James Brittain/ VIEW; 152 - 153 Darren Chung/ James Noble/ designer and maker of unique wagons www.wiltshirewagons.co.uk; 154 – 155 Guy Mallinson/ www.mallinson.co.uk; 157 above left Philiy Page/ The Yurt Retreat, Somerset www.theyurtretreat.co.uk; 157 above right John Warburton-Lee Photography/ Alamy; 157 below left www.Mermeladaestudio.es/ Angela Moore; 157 below right MTUNDERCANVAS; 158 left Philiy Page/ The Yurt Retreat, Somerset www.theyurtretreat.co.uk; 158 right Yellowstone Under Canvas; 159 above left The Interior Archive/ Tandem Photography; 159 above right The Interior Archive/ Tandem Photography; 159 below Paperbark Camp/ Photographer: Dick Sweeney; 160 Guy Mallinson/ www.mallinson.co.uk; 161 above The Interior Archive/ Tim Beddow; 161 below Yellowstone Under Canvas; 162 above & below www.ipcsyndication.com; 163 Kristin Perers Copyright Country Living/ Hearst Magazines UK: 164 – 165 Guy Mallinson/ www.mallinson.co.uk; 166 GDM Limited/ MetroShip; 167 Corbis; 169 above left www.sealander.de; 169 above right Corbis; 169 below left Corbis; 169 below right Getty; 170 Corbis; 171 Getty; 172 above & below GDM Limited/ MetroShip; 173 above & below Navid Baraty; 174 - 175 Ray Main/ Mainstreamimages/ Jim Thompson; 176 - 179 Andreas von Einsiedel/ Bryony Hebson; 180 - 181 www.ipcsyndication.com; 182 - 185 Michele Turriani; 186 Narratives / Photo: Claire Richardson; 188 left The Interior Archive/ William Waldron; 188 right Robin Falck, Helsinki, industrial based designer; 189 left Franck Schmitt/ Oredia/ Lived In Images; 189 right Michele Turriani; 190 above left The Interior Archive/ Sebastian Siraudeau; 190 above right James Merrell Copyright Country Living/ Hearst Magazines UK; 190 below left Evan Sklar/ Red Cover/ Photoshot; 190 below right www.ipcsyndication.com; 191 left Andreas von Einsiedel/ Axel Vervoordt; 191 right Main/ Mainstreamimages/ Baileyshomeandgarden.com; 192 left Simon Bevan Copyright Country Living/ Hearst Magazines UK; 192 right Andreas von Einsiedel/ Bryony Hebson; 193 above left Andreas von Einsiedel/ Axel Vervoordt; 193 above right The Interior Archive/ Nicolas Matheus; 193 below Douglas Gibb/ Red Cover/ Photoshot; 194 left www.edwardscobbuilding.com/ www.cobcourses.com; 194 right Jacqui Small LLP; 195 above left Taverneagency.com/ Photographer: Mikkel Vang; 195 above right Richard Powers; 195 below left Country Living/ Hearst Magazines UK; 195 below right Alun Callender Copyright Country Living/ Hearst Magazines UK; 196 left The Interior Archive/ Nicolas Matheus; 196 right The Interior Archive/ Roger Davies/ Designer and Owner Jane Hallworth; 197 above left Jake Fitzjones Photography/ Claire Peters; 197 above right Jacqui Small LLP; 197 below Bodrifty Roundhouse, available to hire from www.hiddenhideaways.co.uk/ Photographer: Ian Kingsnorth; 198 above left Narratives/ Photo: A. Mezza & E. Escalante / Owner: Cartucho Antoraz & Susana Bárcena; 198 above right The Interior Archive/ Roger Davies/ Designer and Owner Jane Hallworth; 198 below To book a stay at The Beer Moth go to www.canopyandstars.co.uk/Photographer: Sophie

Burry; 199 left www.ipcsyndication.com; 199 right The Interior Archive/ Alex Ramsay; 200 left Taverneagency.com/ Photographer: Anouk de Kleermaeker/ Producer: Hanneke de Jager; 200 right Taverneagency.com/ Photographer: Robbert Koene / Producer: Liezel Norval-Kruger; 201 Taverneagency. com/ Photographer: Colin Cooke/ Producer: Paul Lowe;

FRONT COVER: Jake Fitzjones Photography/ Claire Peters.

BACK COVER: above left www.duntonhotsprings. com; above centre James Brittain/ VIEW; above right Getty; below left Photo: Peter Lundstrom, WDO - www.treehotel.se; below centre Paul Massey/ Mainstreamimages; below right Guy Mallinson/ www.mallinson.co.uk;

ENDPAPERS: Left to right: Guy Mallinson/ www. mallinson.co.uk; Alchemy LLC; Pierre Stephane Dumas/ www.BubbleTree.fr; Lakes Cottage Holidays; Country Living/ Hearst Magazines UK; Sindabezi Island, Livingstone, Zambia www. tongabezi.com; www.duntonhotsprings.com; Getty; Tongabezi Lodge, Livingstone, Zambia www.tongabezi.com; The Interior Archive/ Andrew Wood; The Interior Archive/ Simon Upton; FREE SPIRIT SPHERES Inc.; Bodrifty Roundhouse, available to hire from www.hiddenhideaways.co.uk/ Photographer: Ian Kingsnorth; Interior Archive/ Simon Upton; Jacqui Small LLP:

Author Acknowledgements

With special thanks to Jacqui Small and Jo Copestick for their direction and guidance, to Sian Parkhouse for being at the end of the phone and email, and for keeping it all in order and to Ashley Western and Claire Hamilton for making this such a visually appealing book. Also to AWJ for the tea and understanding.